# eat london

D1635511

**architecture and eating**

samantha hardingham
photographs by keith collie

# eat london

architecture and eating

• • • ellipsis

British Library cataloguing in publication
A CIP record for this book is available from the British Library

PUBLISHED BY •••ellipsis
2 Rufus Street London N1 6PE
E MAIL ...@ellipsis.co.uk
WWW http://www.ellipsis.com
SERIES EDITOR Tom Neville
SERIES DESIGN Jonathan Moberly

COPYRIGHT © 1999 Ellipsis London Limited
ISBN 1 84166 003 5

FILM PROCESSING METRO IMAGING

PRINTING AND BINDING Hong Kong

•••ellipsis is a trademark of Ellipsis
London Limited

For a copy of the Ellipsis catalogue or
information on special quantity orders
of Ellipsis books please contact
Lindsay Evans
0171–739 3157 or lindsay@ellipsis.co.uk

eat london: architecture eating and drinking

**Samantha Hardingham 1999**

# Contents

# Introduction

A RESTAURANT EXAMINED

The interior of a restaurant, examined in some detail, offers the keen eye of the philosopher a spectacle well worth his interest, on account of the variety of situations contained within it.

The far end of the room is occupied by a host of solitary diners, who order loudly, wait impatiently, eat rapidly, pay and depart.

At another table is a family from the country, content with a frugal meal, yet relishing one or two unfamiliar dishes, and obviously enjoying the novelty of their surroundings.

Nearby sit a husband and wife, Parisians, from the evidence of the hat and shawl hanging nearby; it is clearly a long time since they had anything to say to each other; they are going to the theatre, and it is a safe bet that one of them will fall asleep during the performance.

Farther on are two lovers, judging by the attentions of one, the coquetry of the other, and the gourmandism of both. Pleasure shines in their eyes; and, from the choice that governs the composition of their meal, the present serves both to illuminate the past and foreshadow the future.

In the centre of the room is a table surrounded by regular patrons, who as a rule obtain special terms, and dine at a fixed price. They know the names of all the waiters; who let them into the secret of what is freshest and newest; they are like the stock-in-trade of a shop, like a centre of attraction, or to be more precise, like the decoys used in Brittany to attract wild duck.

There are also a number of individuals who everyone knows by sight, and no one by name. These people are as much at ease as if they were at home, and quite often try and strike up a conversation with their neighbours. They belong to a type met with only in Paris, which has neither property, capital, nor employment, but spends freely for all that.

Finally, there are one or two foreigners, usually Englishmen; these last stuff themselves with double portions, order all the most expensive dishes, drink the headiest wines, and do not always leave without assistance.

The accuracy of our description may be verified any day of the week; and if it succeeds in rousing curiosity, perhaps it may also serve as a moral warning.

From *The Physiology of Taste*, Jean-Anthelme Brillat-Savarin (1825)

If one examines a restaurant today, the situation barely differs, but there would be additional items to enhance a picture for the late 1990s. Perhaps if he were alive today Brillat-Savarin might have expanded his comment to include, 'Tell me what you eat (*and where*) and I will tell you what you are'. There are restaurants in London today to satisfy everyone from gourmands to gluttons, every palate from Arkansas to Afghanistan, every mood from canteen to cantina and increasingly at almost any time of day. Coffee bars and cafés have taken hold of the city in the last three years, and now no museum, gallery or store is complete without its own restaurant.

London has recently been acclaimed as 'the restaurant capital of the world'. The city's title is based on a new-found design-consciousness which has made an impact on everything from home decoration and gardening to cooking at home and eating out. Elsewhere, the concept of eating out has been integrated into the infrastructure of the city for a long time, and has therefore reached a level of sophistication. Of course,

# Introduction

France lays claim to the first restaurant but the culture is also inside every single New Yorker, whether they are ordering Chinese food to go or drinking a martini at the Four Seasons. The key to this is the fact that service is taken very seriously in the US – it is by no means regarded as a menial job. In Asian countries, the range of ingredients may be more specific and the kitchen made of scrap, but you could not reproduce a more refined culture of street cooking in any restaurant.

London's gastronomic roots are embedded in the public house which would serve ale and victuals (to men *and* women) and often have boarding rooms for travellers (an inn). The oldest pub still standing in London today is The George Inn at 77 Borough High Street, SE1, the only galleried coaching inn left in the city. The present pub was built in 1676 but stands on the site of an inn which dates back to 1542. It now belongs to the National Trust. In the City, merchants and bankers would dine in chop houses which were much closer to our contemporary idea of a restaurant. The Quality Chop House at 94 Farringdon Road, EC1, is a fine example and still intact, although it has recently expanded to include a fish restaurant. More artistic and scholarly types would meet in coffee houses (host to countless societies) which would stay open as long as there were customers to serve. The first recorded coffee house was established in 1652 in Cornhill in the City (when coffee arrived in this country). Chocolate appeared in England at around the same time so there were even one or two chocolate houses.

Recently we have witnessed the redefinition of the pub in response to the cultural shift towards leisure and more flexible working hours for both men and women, rather than a 9-to-5 day for the husband with a stop off at the pub for a pint on the way home. The Eagle at 159 Farringdon Road, EC1, is acclaimed as London's first 'gastropub', where all its Victorian trappings (island bar and upholstery) have been stripped out, leaving timber floors, replacing obscured glass windows with clear panes, a miss-matched assortment of old wooden chairs and tables and a long bar along one wall which also serves as an open kitchen producing energetic, hearty Mediterranean food. The model has been copied all over London and has swept away the old conventions of 'the public bar' (for workmen in grubby overalls – often this side of the bar had a wooden or concrete floor) and 'the saloon bar' (for ladies and gents – carpeted). The first *organic* gastro-pub opened this year at the Duke of Cambridge, 30 St Peter's Street, N1. Many breweries now own large chains of bar-pubs which are designed to attract a younger 20-to-30-something audience: The Slug & Lettuce, The Pitcher & Piano, All Bar One, O'Neill's, Hogshead and Ferret & Firkin pubs can be found all over town. But while the new pub appeals to the marketing-man's definition of this sector of society, the 'No Dirty Overalls' signs on the windows of London's remaining 'drinking pubs' exclude another sector entirely.

Design has proved to be divisive in the evolution of our bars, but this is more to do with the business of selling a lifestyle than it is to do with developing a building type. In 1976 a firm called Kennedy Brookes, started by accountant Michael Golder and businessman Roy Ackerman, went into the business of rationalising menus and management procedures in small- to medium-sized restaurants, reducing every aspect to its most profitable essentials. They started with motorway service stations and went on to control more than 50 restaurants (see Bertorelli's, formerly Cafe Italien des Amis du Vin, page 9.4), aiming to give each one an individual look in order to maintain an 'at-home' quality but all operating under one corporate umbrella. The designers Virgile and Stone (then at Fitch) designed the concepts for many of Kennedy Brookes' Soho and

eat london: architecture and eating

## Introduction

Fitzrovia restaurants. The presence of Kennedy Brookes on the restaurant scene forced London's restaurateurs either to follow the approach or to take an even more personal hand in presenting food and setting. The likes of Terence Conran, Alastair Little and Stephen Bull have all matched their surroundings with their culinary opinions but even so V & S have since gone on to specialise in design for these individual tastes (see Stephen Bull, St Martin's Lane, page 3.2).

There is a long tradition of architects not only designing restaurants but also opening their own establishments (see 192 on page 1.22 and St John on page 3.10). The relationship between the two disciplines is intimate with their shared fascination with detail, materials, a pleasure in indulging the senses and the sociable desire to create a community and a spectacle. The most significant of recent developments in this direction has been the emergence of the mega-restaurant. This is the restaurant industry's and the architectural profession's version of BritPop and BritArt. A theatrical flair for large-scale operations has been present in restaurant design in this country for some time. The Lyons Corner House at Coventry Street was built in 1907 to the designs of W J Ancell (see the Atlantic Bar & Grill, page 5.2) and could seat up to 4500 people over several floors. La Belle Epoque (see page 4.14), seating a mere 800, is London's largest establishment to date, but the principle has been maintained – that of encompassing several different types of restaurant, brasserie, cocktail bar (and therefore different-sized budgets) under one roof. The mega-restaurant has been a playground for clients to enter into big business (often partnerships comprising an accountant, a restaurateur and a celebrity chef), for fashion designers to create uniforms and costumes for the staff, and, for architects to indulge in wild frivolity or experiment with prototypes and architectural devices (see Bank on page

4.8 and Belgo Centraal on page 10.6) in the controlled conditions of a restaurant interior. The building type provides a fast turnover of production that a more complete building project cannot accommodate or sustain. Frivolity often takes the form of nostalgia and in big business this means big bucks. Although Terence Conran (see pages 2.2–2.4) has broken new ground (many restaurateurs say that he single-handedly brought the capital out of the recession of the late 1980s by developing previously neglected areas and giving Londoners the confidence to dine out *en masse*), the design of his restaurants harks back romantically to another era.

Our eating habits have been deeply influenced by the rich mix of ethnic cooking brought here by the many different immigrant populations that have settled in London over the years, from our anglicised curries (see PukkaBar, page 11.10) to kebabs. The early 1990s saw architects and restaurateurs trying to capture the essence of traditional methods of cooking and eating while encompassing the increasingly eclectic skills of chefs and designers to make the experience relevant to our own contemporary situation. Often this process of purification and distillation has resulted in a so-called 'minimal' interior (often mistaken for 'modern') whereby the architect has bleached out the space in order to focus on the food and the people. Certain cultures lend themselves to this type of rationalisation – as in John Pawson's conceptual treatment of Wagamama (see page 10.22). Others are more contrived to develop the idea of the interior space and activity within as more of a sculptural form which in turn shares a relationship with the street (see Coast on page 3.20 and Momo on page 11.2).

Whether a restaurant sinks or swims is essentially the result of a balance between excellence of food, service and design. In this volatile

**eat london: architecture and eating**

and competitive climate where customers have learned to demand more and more for their money, expectations are high and these criteria become even more inextricably linked. Unless a small local restaurant is firmly imprinted with the attentive hand of its proprietor (see Sonny's, page 8.32), many customers will opt for a more stimulating night out at one of the many breathtaking or unusual locations that are now readily available. Visiting a restaurant has become as viable a proposition as a trip to the theatre (and one would expect to pay as much in the more theatrical establishments). No doubt we shall find out sooner rather than later where this tide will take us although, as history teaches us, good design and thorough attention to detail will undoubtedly weather the storm. In the first edition of this book my hunch was that the local restaurant, given new confidence, would make a comeback (see One Lawn Terrace, page 8.18) but this time will be nurtured by the high standards set by the bigger establishments and a heightened epicurean vocabulary.

All the bars and coffee bars that appeared in the first edition of this guide have been extracted because they now constitute a book in themselves (*drink london*). New entries this year reveal that on the basis of the success of their first venture, many restaurants have gone on to develop further sites (see Konditor & Cook on page 8.28 and YO!Sushi on page 6.2), becoming small chains. Some restaurateurs continue to explore types of cuisine and therefore new ways of making restaurants and new places to put them (see PukkaBar on page 11.10 and Great Eastern Dining Room, page 8.20).

1998/99 has been The Year of the Buy-Out. Large organisations such as the Belgo Group have swallowed up the likes of The Ivy and Le Caprice (although the original owners remain in key management positions). The stakes are high and the chips are down for Groupe Chez Gerard who ate various establishments such as Livebait and Richoux for breakfast while continuing to develop new sites bearing the Chez Gerard name. Star chefs such as Marco Pierre White – in pursuit of the mega-site to out-do and out-glamorise all mega-sites (see Titanic, page 3.36) – are on the verge of turning a theme into high-art. Designers such as David Collins and United Designers have perfected their art through this kind of mass expansion.

This book aims to show a particular direction that some restaurants have chosen to take by describing a key influence on their success or failure: that of design, and, consequently how that determines the way we are eating out in 1999. Design emerges in more than just an interior – it is embedded in the underlying motivation for any restaurant whether it be high-concept or pure passion. Places have been selected which illustrate the extremes. The section headings explain the story of how, as a building type, the restaurant presents itself today.

SH February 1999

**eat london: architecture and eating**

# Pricing

Prices are strictly a guide, indicating an average per head for a three-course dinner with half a bottle of wine. In many of the more expensive restaurants it is cheaper to eat at lunchtime; there is often a set lunch during the week or a brunch menu at weekends.

EXPENSIVE £40–£50
The Avenue
Le Caprice
Che
Circus
City Rhodes
Coast
Le Coq d'Argent
The Criterion
5th Floor at Harvey Nichols (restaurant)
The Ivy
Nobu
Oxo Tower Restaurant
Putney Bridge
The River Café
Thomas Goode
Quo Vadis
Wakaba

A LITTLE MORE THAN MODERATE £30–£40
Alfred

Alastair Little
Bank
La Belle Epoque
Cicada
Euphorium
Granita
Kensington Place
Mash
Mezzo Restaurant
Momo
Moro
One Lawn Terrace
192
The People's Palace
Polygon Bar & Grill
Quaglino's
St John
Scotts
Sonny's
Stephen Bull's Bistro
Stephen Bull, St Martin's Lane
Villandry

MODERATE £20–£30
AKA
Atlantic Bar & Grill (drinks only)
Belgo Noord
Belgo Centraal
Bertorelli's
Bluebird
Chez Gerard
East One
5th Floor at Harvey Nichols
(brasserie)
Great Eastern Dining Room
Mezzonine

Noho
Oxo Tower Brasserie
R K Stanley's
Titanic
Zinc Bar & Grill

CHEAP £10–£20
Eco
Konditor & Cook
Pizza Express
Wagamama
YO!Sushi

eat london: architecture and eating

# pioneers

# Scott's

Elegance, glamour, style, dazzle and panache are all epithets which have been applied to Scott's. The legend began in Leicester Square where Mr John Scott sold oysters from a wheelbarrow at a penny a throw. He went on to open his Oyster Warehouse in 1851 on the corner of Haymarket and Piccadilly (now the site of Sogo, the Japanese department store). By the 1890s Scott's had moved to Mount Street, where it was host to Edward, Prince of Wales, and Lily Langtry. It continued to flourish throughout the 1920s and '30s, attracting film stars such as Clark Gable and Marlene Dietrich, and even managed to maintain standards during two world wars. The restaurant takes its place in movie history too – in the dreams of two prisoners of war in *The Great Escape* – and it was in this bar that James Bond author Ian Fleming asked for his Martini to be 'shaken not stirred'.

In 1994 the restaurant was acquired by the Groupe Chez Gerard, who instigated the radical refurbishment of the interior. The new owners felt that the restaurant had 'lost some of its innate style over the years' (including the loss of a substantial art collection which left with the previous owner). The architect's brief was to 'relaunch Scott's with a new image drawn from its glamorous heyday' – so while the ambience is contemporary, there are period elements which evoke an art-deco feel. The most sensitive of these features are the decorative plaster chandelier in the foyer and the frieze behind the raw bar by Oriel Harwood. A bubble column – centrepiece of the glass spiral staircase connecting the ground-floor restaurant and basement cocktail bar – is a late 20th-century feature. Although serving as a plinth for a magnificent flower arrangement, the column feels strangely isolated in the somewhat over-rationalised space. Whereas at one time the main ground-floor room was dimly illuminated by an artificially backlit skylight, and the space broken up by well-worn

**Peter Leonard 1997**

**Peter Leonard 1997**

leather banquette seats and deep comfortable chairs, now it has notionally been divided in two and sprayed with halogen spotlights. The front area, the Oyster Terrace, opens out on to the street. A cool, marble floor, table tops embedded with fossils of shellfish, and newly designed wooden chairs decorate the interior and the pavement area which has deep awnings. The main restaurant has been pushed towards the back of the space (where the skylight has been retained) and diners are penned into a carpeted *à la carte* corral.

The long, low bar in the basement snakes along one wall; gold with a black surface. The room is lit by the energising glow emanating from the bottle bank behind the bar, with tints of Gordon's green and Martell gold. Under the pavement, curtained recesses make intimate private rooms for discreet liaisons.

The frontage remains remarkably intact: the large round window is still a focal point, and the canopied gilt and mahogany entrance doors and stone-clad tradesman's lift concealed in the facia are still in use. A refurbishment such as this is an unenviable task as it can only serve to upset those who felt so comfortable in the charm of the original setting. The process of patination must now begin all over again.

ADDRESS 20 Mount Street, London W1 (0171–629 5248)
CLIENT Groupe Chez Gerard (L Isaacson and N Abraham)
SIZE 880 square metres including kitchens
SEATS 110 plus 35 in Oyster Terrace
OPEN restaurant Monday–Friday, 12.00–15.00, 18.00–23.00; Saturday, 18.00–23.00; Sunday, 11.30–16.00, 19.00–22.00. Oyster Terrace 12.00–16.00, 18.00–23.00; Sunday, 11.30–16.00, 19.00–22.00
UNDERGROUND Green Park, Bond Street, Hyde Park Corner

pioneers

Peter Leonard 1997

# The Ivy

The Ivy and its sister restaurant Le Caprice (see page 1.10) have been inextricably linked since 1947. The man behind the success of both was Mario Gallati, who came to London from Broni near Milan at the age of fourteen in 1903. His progress led from the kitchen sink of his Bayswater lodgings via the Savoy to the door of Abel Giandellini who owned a modest café on West Street, The Ivy. 'The place made a poor impression' on Gallati but he was encouraged to stay when Abel bought the whole corner site and handed control of the kitchen to him. Gallati said that 'The Ivy was lucky from the start' – the café was close to the theatres and became very popular with actors, directors and theatre-goers (everyone from Churchill to Puccini came to dine). It also undoubtedly benefited from Gallati's professionalism in the kitchen and his sympathetic manner with the customers.

By 1928 the building was in such disrepair that it had to be demolished and rebuilt to include a dining room upstairs, becoming one of the most valuable freeholds in the West End. The customers could not bear to be without their Ivy, so during the rebuild Gallati continued to serve spaghetti despite open walls, holes in the floor and no heating. Patrons would sit stoically in fur coats and scarves, and occasionally with umbrellas.

Twenty-eight years later, an increasingly strained relationship with the proprietor forced Gallati to leave. He opened Le Caprice, taking many of his customers with him. Between his departure and the acquisition of The Ivy by Corbin and King in 1989, it passed through several hands (including Wheelers in 1950). Corbin and King had owned Le Caprice since 1981 so once again the two restaurants were united.

Today, The Ivy retains the atmosphere of the timber-panelled Regency-style dining room. The triangular leaded stained-glass windows on both the West Street and Litchfield Street sides may have belonged to the orig-

**Long & Kentish 1990**

**Long & Kentish 1990**

inal restaurant (c. 1928), but almost certainly to the previous occupant, Wheelers. Stripped back to the brick in the 1990 refurbishment by Long & Kentish, the tired timber was reinstated in a new form – the detailing is to be admired. However, the real innovation is in the cast-plaster ceiling which acts as a giant light fitting and replaces the fiddly wall lights of the original restaurant. An old chair found in the changing rooms of Le Caprice was used as a model for the restaurant chairs.

The other significant new contribution to the rooms derives from architect M J Long's close association with many leading contemporary artists, and Corbin and King's admiration for the art and crafts collections at Mr Chow's restaurant in Knightsbridge and Corbin's former employer, the late Peter Langan. Artists (all customers) commissioned to create site-specific works include David Bailey, Clive Barker, Peter Blake, Patrick Caulfield, Barry Flanagan, David Gryn, Sir Howard Hodgin, Bill Jacklin, Allen Jones, Michael Craig-Martin, Janet Nathan, Sir Eduardo Paolozzi, Tom Phillips, Liz Rideal and Joe Tilson. Future Systems (architects of King's own home in Islington – now sold) designed the champagne bucket and dessert trolley. The front door on the West Street side has recently been replaced and the art collection continues to evolve.

Gallati observed that although the English may appear to be cold and unfriendly they do take people and places to their hearts – The Ivy is one of those places.

ADDRESS 1–5 West Street, London WC2 (0171–836 4751)
CLIENTS Chris Corbin and Jeremy King (Caprice Holdings)
SIZE 700 square metres on three floors SEATS approximately 120
OPEN 12.00–15.00 (Sunday –15.30), 17.30–24.00
UNDERGROUND Leicester Square

**Long & Kentish 1990**

Long & Kentish 1990

# Le Caprice

The restaurant is on the ground floor of an apartment block designed by Michael Rosenauer in 1936, at the end of a discrete cul-de-sac behind the Ritz hotel. The building is typical of a period when facilities such as shops, hairdressers and restaurants were often integrated into the design of residential developments (Dolphin Square, SW1, built in 1937 and the White House, NW1, built in 1936, expand on this idea). Today's establishment takes its name from the restaurant which had occupied the site between 1947 and 1975 (prior to that it had been called Corvette, Arlington, Quintos and Cicogne). It is inspired by and still thrives off the reputation of its distinguished proprietor during that period, Mario Gallati. (For the story of how Le Caprice became inextricably linked to its big sister, The Ivy, see page 1.6.)

Le Caprice reopened in 1981 under a new guise created by restaurateurs Chris Corbin and Jeremy King with designer and retailer Joseph Ettedgui and architect Eva Jiricna.

King gained much of his restaurant experience at Joe Allen in Exeter Street, WC2, while developing a love for the excitement of London's theatre district. Corbin was greatly inspired by a stint at Langan's; the late Peter Langan's legendary brasserie in Stratton Street, W1. It was here that Joseph (a regular customer) proposed the Le Caprice venture to Corbin. Joseph withdrew from the project only four months after opening (due to a conflict about the direction the restaurant should take), but he had been expert in identifying the moment and the site and introducing Eva Jiricna as architect.

Working with a very small budget, Jiricna retained many of existing features but applied new materials and lighting to develop a modernist look for Le Caprice which would sit happily inside the 1930s shell. The comfortable bar stools which had previously been swathed in brown

**Eva Jiricna Architects 1981**

**Eva Jiricna Architects 1981**

velvet were recovered in black leather. The main investment was in the Italian black tiled floor. Lighting is indirect and concealed in cornice details and in fittings mounted to mirrors. The life-saver-shaped light fittings, designed by Jiricna, are simple black brackets holding frosted Perspex rings over fluorescent tubes.

The cream walls, hung with artists' prints and photographs, are highlighted with chrome and mirrored glass to smoulder like Lauren Bacall in a Dior dress. Silver Venetian blinds permit only a limited view into the restaurant from the pavement, adding to the seductiveness of Le Caprice, which has retained a glistening, understated aura.

Le Caprice has long been established as one of the most consummate restaurants in London. Like The Ivy, it attracts every film star, politician, author and artist that anyone might care to mention. Gallati said that during his 60 years of working in the restaurant business, he found 'the greatest connoisseurs of good food are amongst members of the medical profession!' Corbin and King have continued to maintain the very personal contact that Gallati established with all his customers.

A new entrance canopy designed by Jiricna is now in place. The chrome wedge over the door is more pediment than shelter.

ADDRESS Arlington House, Arlington Street, London SW1
(0171-629 2239)
CLIENTS Chris Corbin, Jeremy King, Joseph Ettedgui
BUDGET £20,000
SIZE approximately 200 square metres SEATS 70
OPEN 12.00–15.00 (Sunday –15.30), 17.30–24.00
UNDERGROUND Green Park

**Eva Jiricna Architects 1981**

Le Caprice

pioneers

**Eva Jiricna Architects 1981**

# The River Cafe

The earth-shattering success of the *The River Cafe Cookbook* (volumes 1 and 2) seems only to boost the profile of the restaurant. Now that many of the most popular recipes are available in print, and some supermarkets have responded by stocking the ingredients, the restaurant can remain the domain of the very rich and the very famous. Renowned as the best Italian food outside of Italy, it may also be the most expensive.

Richard Rogers' Italian roots and personal design philosophy are evident in the planning of the site. The restaurant is located within his office compound, creating a social focus and public facility for the working community. In restaurant speak, the location is a 'destination site' – obscure, set back from the road, away from any other retail or restaurant activity, making it the perfect getaway for bashful superstars.

Occupying the ground floor of one of the Victorian brick warehouses, the transformation from warehouse to restaurant has not been a demonstrative exercise for Rogers, or used as a test-bed for his more radical ideas. It is a simple conversion which has maintained all of the light-filled, spacious qualities of the original interiors. Large windows line the front of the space and look south on to a landscaped area and the river.

'Deliberately conceived along domestic lines, with a small open kitchen, a menu that would change daily, and the unconventional idea that the waiters and kitchen porters would be involved in the preparation of the food' – these are the proprietors' ideals. The result is larger and more sophisticated than one would imagine from such a modest description. The main feature of the white-walled space, and hub for all activity, is the 15-metre-long counter at the back of the room. The stainless steel top with mirrored front serves as the bar and a preparation area, with a wood-burning stove at one end encased in crisp stainless steel panelling. The angled glass screens above the bar reflect and deflect light and noise.

**Richard Rogers Partnership 1987**

pioneers

# The River Cafe

White clothed tables fill the room, matched with the modern classic chair (in wood, chrome and cane) designed by Marcel Breuer in the 1930s. The main kitchen lies beyond the fireplace wall in order to benefit from natural light and the river aspect.

The shadow clock on the wall is a quintessential expression of the restraint which has been applied to the overall design. Each element or function has been designed as a simple gesture, while the materials used underline the nature of each activity.

The kitchen has not only been a breeding ground for dynamic young chefs; its philosophy has also inspired a genre of restaurant design.

ADDRESS Thames Wharf Studios, Rainville Road, London W6 (0171–381 8824)
CLIENTS Ruth Rogers and Rose Gray
SIZE restaurant 130 square metres; kitchen 110 square metres
SEATS approximately 110
OPEN Monday–Saturday, 12.30–15.00 (last orders 14.15), 19.00–23.00 (last orders 21.30); Sunday, 12.30–15.00 (last orders 14.15)
UNDERGROUND Hammersmith

**Richard Rogers Partnership 1987**

**Richard Rogers Partnership 1987**

# Stephen Bull's Bistro

At 27 years old, while managing accounts at an advertising agency, Stephen Bull thought it was time for a dramatic career change. One of his clients at the time was Olivetti which meant frequent trips to Italy and long lunches – ultimately the source of his inspiration to become a chef. Bull, entirely self-taught with a just a spate in Peter Langan's kitchen, now has three successful restaurants in London. The first opened in Blandford Street in 1989 (for the third, in St Martin's Lane, see page 3.2). Stephen Bull is gravely serious about his craft but he is also at ease with it – an attitude which is reflected in the design of his restaurants. Like each dish that he serves, each restaurant is composed of its own set of ingredients (location, type of building, people) so the result is always different. He is one of the currently less-fashionable generation of restaurateurs who has a refined understanding of dining out – an experience which can be relaxing and sophisticated and, sometimes, an education. He acknowledges the mega-restaurant trade as being aimed towards a younger crowd who are seduced by the 'fun-orientated' locations, but finds it 'vulgar' in its single-minded pursuit of their purses.

Stephen Bull's Bistro opened in Clerkenwell in 1992. It was an untried venture in relatively unknown territory. He recognised that the area was about to undergo a huge demographic shift – following the New York trend to convert light-industrial buildings into loft-style living space for young professional residents (a process which is now well under way). At the time, Bull was breaking new ground by combining his seminal food with a personal enthusiasm for modern architecture. The Bistro was a new kind of cosmopolitan restaurant – today, it is an integral part of the city.

Initially the site was the poorly lit, narrow ground-floor area of a 19th century building with a very deep entrance corridor. Allies & Morrison cut through the back of the space up to the first floor to create a mezzanine

**Allies & Morrison 1992**

**Stephen Bull's Bistro**

**pioneers**

**Allies & Morrison 1992**

and allow natural light in through rooflights. They carved sideways to bring a larger area of the restaurant up to the street, allowing light through the front of the building and revealing more of the activity inside. Planes of strong colour and light run through the interior excavation to connect visually the different spaces upstairs and on the ground floor. Any additional decoration has been applied to set-piece details such as the bent-steel staircase which leads up to the mezzanine seating, the coat rails (with meat hooks), the aluminium dado, and the curved maple screen balustrade upstairs which obscures diners from downstairs and serves as a rack for hats, coats and bags. The *papier-mâché* sculptures by Sarah Williams have been added by Bull's own capricious hand.

Bull admits that the layout of the building is not ideal for a restaurant: he considers the deep entrance to be a waste of space and the constraints of the site forced the kitchen to be sited on two floors, which is inefficient. In spite of these inconveniences and in response to the increasing popularity for new restaurant openings in the area, Bull has recently introduced a bar into one side of the plan, thus making the restaurant more contained (therefore easier to observe and manage), leaving the variety of spaces, the generous height throughout and the simplicity of detailing intact.

ADDRESS 71 St John Street, London EC1 (0171–490 1750)
ENGINEER Price & Myers
CLIENT Stephen Bull
SIZE ground-floor restaurant 112 square metres; mezzanine floor 56 square metres; bar 60 square metres SEATS 120
OPEN Monday–Friday, 12.00–14.30, 18.00–22.30; Saturday, 19.00–22.30 (closed bank holidays)
UNDERGROUND Farringdon

**Allies & Morrison 1992**

**pioneers**

**Allies & Morrison 1992**

# 192

The origins of many a bar or restaurant lie in the desire of their creators to make a social centre for their own community. The concept for this 'neighbourhood drop-in' follows the partners' other ventures – Zanzibar (1973; now deceased) and the Groucho Club – and brings together John Amit's wine expertise, Tony Mackintosh's management style, and Tchaik Chassay's design, also seen at the Jazz Café and Granita (see page 8.8), making for a devastatingly trendy and sociable hang-out – the banquette seat being the primary device with which to procure such an environment.

The initial idea (and a reflection of the early 1980s) was for a ground-floor wine bar with seating in the basement. However, in the late 1980s, Alastair Little brought 'serious food' out of the kitchen, initiating a stable of first-rate chefs and expansion into the next-door building.

Chassay believes in an equal balance between design, food and management, although the current climate has stimulated 'people to expect to spend a lot of money and get something back: excitement, glamour, warmth – and in large quantities'. As long as 192 remains under current ownership (and there is no reason why this should change) it will fulfil its original function and maintain its reputation as a refuge for Notting Hill Gate's trustafarian set whose purses are impervious to dramatic changes in fashion and whose purpose in life is to hang-out.

ADDRESS 192 Kensington Park Road, London W11 (0171–229 0482)
CLIENTS John Amit, Tony Mackintosh, Tchaik Chassay
SIZE approximately 300 square metres
SEATS 120
OPEN 12.30–15.00 (Saturday and Sunday, 12.30–15.30), 19.00–23.30 (Sunday, 19.00–23.00)
UNDERGROUND Ladbroke Grove, Notting Hill Gate

**Chassay Architects 1984, extended in 1993**

**Chassay Architects 1984, extended in 1993**

# Kensington Place

> The arrival of the restaurant as a building type, rather than as the domain of the decorator, was announced by Julyan Wickham's Kensington Place ... This establishment has, more than any other, been the culinary and architectural model for those which have followed over the past decade.
>
> Jonathan Meades, 'Making a meal of it', *Perspectives*, February/ March 1997

Wickham has combined different elements from European schools of design into an overall scheme to update a popular concept of the French brasserie. What sounds like plagiarism is in fact a creative strain which has become peculiar to the architect. The principles underlying the proclamation of the Weimar Bauhaus in 1919, as outlined by Bruno Taut, stated that 'there will be no boundaries between the crafts, sculpture and painting; all will be one: Architecture'. Walter Gropius elaborated by calling for artists to return to crafts, 'to go into buildings, endow them with fairy tales ... and build in fantasy without regard for technical ability'. This idea is more developed in Wickham's later work at Bank (see page 4.8), but the beginnings of an integrated design can be seen here.

There is a toughness about the choice of this ground-floor site. It adheres to the 1960s office block in which it is set and confronts the busy pedestrian and vehicular traffic outside. The bold and simple gesture of glazing the ground-floor façade has opened up a relationship between the interior and the street which could not otherwise have been attained. The restaurant can by no means be described as an entirely steel and glass structure, but the lightness of the street façade alone (down to the use of steel Crittal window frames) captures the essence of a European architectural expressionism – of the kind illustrated by architect Adolf Behne's

**Wickham & Associates Architects 1987**

**Wickham & Associates Architects 1987**

notion that 'glass architecture will bring a new culture' (1918).

Inside, the warm parquet floor contrasts with the more industrial feel of the three waiters' service-station pylons. These specially designed floor-to-ceiling constructions, which incorporate lighting, shelves for glasses, and cupboards, are located along the middle of the dining room in close proximity to the tables. The stained plywood chairs are to Wickham's own design – a model which has been developed in later projects.

Murals feature largely in Wickham's restaurants. The style and subject matter tend to convey the kind of conventional middle-class happiness indulged in by Impressionists such as Monet and Renoir. The mural here, painted by Wickham's brother Mark, is notable for the absence of people. It contrasts with both the strong architectural forms and notions being expressed in the space and the loud vocal applause of the customers.

ADDRESS 201 Kensington Church Street, London W8 (0171–727 3184)
ENGINEER Dave Cherritt at Knapp Hicks
CLIENT Kensington Place Limited (Nick Smallwood and Simon Slater)
BUDGET £410,000
SIZE 500 square metres
SEATS 140
OPEN 12.00–15.00, 18.30–23.45 (Sunday –22.45)
UNDERGROUND Notting Hill Gate

**Wickham & Associates Architects 1987**

**Wickham & Associates Architects 1987**

# Wakaba

Just as the preparation and enjoyment of Japanese food is a ceremonial activity steeped in tradition, the design of the space in which it is consumed plays a vital role in the ritual. As with the cuisine, there can be no disguising of detail and there are no opportunities for making up for lack of quality with quantity. Wakaba was the first of the Japanese restaurants in London whose design was subjected to a rigorous western minimalism (with Silvestrin and Pawson being its leading exponents). The essence of the activity at hand has been extracted and combined with a few devices to suggest and direct the space.

Wakaba is situated on the ground floor of a 1960s office block on a frantically busy and polluted main road. The curved sand-blasted glass frontage is the only relief from the surrounding chaos – its vulnerability stands out. The gentle curve towards the door draws you into a white walled space. A low wall runs along the side of the space to create a passage so that when customers arrive, rather than streaming into the main dining area in a haphazard fashion, they are directed around the edge of the room.

At a solid counter across the back wall, Mr Yoshihara prepares sushi. The floor is lowered behind the counter, allowing the chef to work easily and customers to sit on comfortable chairs (designed by Hans Werner) rather than perch on bar stools. The wall behind the counter and the side-entrance wall are lined with cupboards in which is stored unsightly clutter such as coats and kitchen utensils.

The 1.5-metre-high wall subdividing the space across the windowed area forms a more private dining room. The height of the wall serves to screen a single row of tables yet allows light in through the front window and into the rest of the space. All the table tops and floor surfaces are made of white-oiled beech, for lightness of colour and softness of texture.

**Claudio Silvestrin and John Pawson 1987**

**Claudio Silvestrin and John Pawson 1987**

## Wakaba

The simple interior composition has since become the model for many a Japanese eating experience in London (see Wagamama, page 10.22). However, the glass façade remains unique; although forming a solid and necessary barrier between inside and outside, it is in harmony with both. Like a flexible membrane, it bows under the pressure of the exterior and appears to balloon outwards from the inside.

ADDRESS 122A Finchley Road, London NW3 (0171–586 7960)
CLIENTS Mr and Mrs Yoshihara
SEATS 55
OPEN Monday to Saturday, 18.30–23.00
UNDERGROUND Finchley Road

**Claudio Silvestrin and John Pawson 1987**

**Claudio Silvestrin and John Pawson 1987**

# the conran hegemony

# The Conran plan

'People don't know what they want until they are offered it.'
Sir Terence Conran

In 1989, when Terence Conran was trying to persuade property developers that the run-down, rat-infested area of Butlers Wharf in Bermondsey had the potential to become a thriving area of shops and restaurants to serve both the City and its own local community, they thought he was barmy. But he was right. There are housing developments by CZWG and Julyan Wickham, and a housing block for 280 students from the London School of Economics – and the Design Museum (1989), based in a radically reconstructed 1950s warehouse overlooking the Thames. Conran's own home is on the top floor of a building designed by Michael Hopkins (1990). His Gastrodrome occupies the entire ground floor of the Butlers Wharf Building, a late-Victorian warehouse with flats on the upper floors.

A quick tour of European cuisine starts at The Chop House, proceeds next door to the Pont de la Tour Restaurant, Bar & Grill, then on to the Cantina del Ponte (a pizza joint), and over to The Blueprint Café at the Design Museum (for more of a sailing-club atmosphere). Windows on the canyon street of Shad Thames reveal the kitchens of each restaurant, as well as an oils and spices shop (a reference to the building's former days as a spice warehouse), a fish shop, a wine merchants, and The Apprentice – a simple canteen restaurant attached to the Butlers Wharf Chefs School. The plans and materials of each restaurant clearly reflect its individual character and suggest the way in which it is used.

Butlers Wharf would not have occurred had it not been driven by the singular vision of Conran Roche (a collaboration between Terence Conran and the late Fred Lloyd Roche, architect) for planning at both

the individual and urban scale. Conran Roche has subsequently become CD Partnership.

What really excites Conran is following a gut feeling and 'seeing the opportunity for an area' – identifying the possibilities of resuscitating a derelict and run-down site and turning it into something useful and special. What he finds incomprehensible is how certain buildings become neglected and apparently obsolete. The great pile of Victorian bricks that is the Great Eastern Hotel, for instance, is in a strategic location and has the potential to serve a vital role in the City. Conran and the CD Partnership, with hotel group Arcadian, are currently renovating and rejuvenating the building.

The redevelopment of the Grade II-listed Michelin House (1986–87), former UK headquarters of the Michelin Tyre Company, set the precedent for Conran's style of urban regeneration and put Brompton Cross on the map. He quotes one of the Michelin brothers when he says that no matter where something is, if it really is good, one will 'make the detour'. For the Michelin brothers, the more detours taken the better it was for their business. Conran's detours may line his own pocket but they also bring areas of the city to life. Today, Michelin House (originally designed by François Espinasse in 1911 and featuring spectacular tiling and stained glass) contains The Conran Shop, Bibendum Restaurant and Oyster Bar, and offices for Reed Consumer Books. It was a collaborative project with publisher Paul Hamlyn.

More recently (1997) a new Conran Shop and The Orrery restaurant have opened at 55–57 Marylebone High Street. An orrery is a clockwork model of the solar system which demonstrates the positions and paths of the planets around the sun: the same model could be used to describe the celestial sphere of Conran's own making. The Orrery is named after

Conran's first restaurant (no longer existing) which opened in 1956 not far from the Bluebird site (page 2.18).

Has he come full circle and is his map complete? I don't suppose so for one moment. Besides the Great Eastern Hotel and several projects in the US, Europe and Japan, there are plans for some smaller restaurants in London. Sartoria is tailor-made for Savile Row, but the most strategic of these sites, geographically and architecturally, is the top-floor restaurant of No. 1 Poultry (aptly named Le Coq d'Argent; see page 2.28).

Design is surprisingly not at the top of Conran's criteria for a good restaurant. First of all he insists that the restaurant must operate efficiently: its kitchen must be a professionally designed work place (not a converted cupboard under the stairs), and the restaurant must be comfortable (for customers who wish to sit for long periods of time and so that members of staff can move around freely) and clean. (Quaglino's never entirely closes down – as soon as the doors close to customers an all-night cleaning programme begins.) Success comes from a 'balanced combination of food, service and design. But without "the buzz" a restaurant is nothing.' Conran suggests that 'the buzz' is as likely to occur in situations that are more spontaneous in terms of their design as in the more self-conscious ventures ... but it all comes back to balance.

Conran's favourite place to eat is 'at home', although he enjoys the buzz at Mezzo and seeing 'spiced-up girls and their grannies' dining there – just as he had imagined it.

# Quaglino's

Giovanni Quaglino came from Piedmont, Italy, to work at the Savoy in London in the early 1920s, alongside the *maître d'hôtel*, Sovrani. The story goes that Sovrani left the hotel to open his own restaurant, taking Giovanni with him. Meanwhile, Sovrani had become rather too enchanted by his employee's wife, so Giovanni repaid this flattery by going into direct competition with Sovrani and taking over the restaurant at the St James's Palace Hotel (later the Hotel Meurice), just around the corner in Bury Street. Thus, Quaglino's was founded in 1929. The main attraction of his restaurant, apart from the exceptional food and gracious service, was a late supper followed by music and dancing. Customers would come especially to listen to Leslie Hutchinson sing Cole Porter numbers. 'Hutch', a Grenadian, was adored by the Mountbattens, Evelyn Waugh, The Prince of Wales, and society women alike. But, above all, Quaglino was the star of his restaurant. By 1935 he was able to buy the whole hotel and his brother Ernest came over to help run the restaurant.

Quaglino's today occupies the hotel ballroom, which was acquired in 1958, by which time the brothers had been retired for several years, although the hotel continued to run well into the 1960s. As the restaurant's brochure says, in the 1930s 'the goal of smart people was, as ever, to be in the same place as even smarter people'. The same could be said of Quaglino's today, for its reincarnation, modelled on the great brasseries in Paris, captures the essence (has even unleashed the spirit) of that illustrious decade.

For all its glamorous spectacle (it was 'designed as a huge, bustling place of entertainment'), Saturday lunchtime is a perfect time to go. This is when staff are at their most relaxed – still fresh in their anticipation of the evening onslaught to come and the prospect of its aftermath. It is also the best time to look at the restaurant itself, because in the evening

**Terence Conran, Keith Hobbs and Linzi Coppick 1993**

**Terence Conran, Keith Hobbs and Linzi Coppick 1993**

the clientele will command your full attention. This is also the perfect time to try and eat in any Conran restaurant. The philosophy that Conran has expounded since the 1960s is one that encourages a nation to feel at home when eating out, while at the same time celebrating the sense of occasion – it's second nature to shell a crab and delight in the fight in public (it's even rather elegant to leave an establishment bespattered with bouillabaisse). The staff live up to the role of a choreographed chorus, dressed by Jasper Conran. His animated uniforms were inspired by the kind of busy French restaurants of the 1940s seen in the 'Tintin' cartoons.

When Conran acquired the premises it was just a big hole in the ground with eight columns nearly 5 metres high running down its length. A mezzanine was inserted to increase floor space and to create a bar area as a prelude to the restaurant. A private dining room to one side overlooks the main dining hall. The dramatic change in level from the entrance down to the bar and then down the rolling stair into the restaurant increases the sense of entering a glittering underworld. This sensation is further uplifted by the new skylight which runs the length of the restaurant. It is, in fact, artificially lit to emulate the change in light from day to night. The light source helps to draw your eye around the whole space as you descend the stairs.

A clear view into the kitchens and wine cellars on the right-hand side reveals some of the specially made kitchen equipment and the meticulous planning of this operation, but not the miles of pipes and ducts which serve to control its micro-climate. All of the furniture, lighting, china and glassware, right down to the detailing of the ashtrays, has been specially designed for the space using solid timber, leather, bronze, nickel, zinc, steel, aluminium and mosaic. The voluptuous double-sided banquette takes centre stage. The aluminium café chairs, with a seat inspired by

**Terence Conran, Keith Hobbs and Linzi Coppick 1993**

**Terence Conran, Keith Hobbs and Linzi Coppick 1993**

Betty Grable's bottom, were originally designed for American prisons. Here they have been given a glossy black finish and dressed with tassels. The careful positioning of these tassels seems to be the basis for a secret code between the staff.

The work of several artists is featured throughout the restaurant and provides the decorative element of the space. The eight columns are the work of Javaid Alvi, Peter Marsh, Philip Hughes, Michael Daykin, Patrick Kinmouth, Catherine Keraly, Jane Harris, and Estelle Thompson. A bas relief by Dhruva Mistry is set in the foyer wall and the mosaic work on the 'crustacea altar' is by Emma Briggs and Tessa Hunkin.

There is a certain brashness in the detailing, and it lacks the sumptuousness of the overall plan. For example, there is an unhappy combination of materials in the 'Q' bannister, and the way that it meets the glass mezzanine barrier at the top is unresolved. On the other hand, Quaglino's is a spatial sensation. Undoubtedly, it fulfils its purpose, able to change from a clattering, train-station-style dining room at lunchtime into a flailing, crazy dance hall at night.

ADDRESS 16 Bury Street, London SW1 (0171–930 6767)
CLIENT Sir Terence Conran with partners Joel Kissin, Keith Hobbs and Tom Conran
SIZE 1500 square metres
SEATS restaurant 275, bar 150
OPEN restaurant: 12.00–14.30, 17.30–23.30; bar: 12.00–23.00
UNDERGROUND Green Park

**Terence Conran, Keith Hobbs and Linzi Coppick 1993**

**Terence Conran, Keith Hobbs and Linzi Coppick 1993**

# Mezzo and Mezzonine

Mezzo was the biggest restaurant in London until La Belle Epoque (see page 4.14) opened with a magnificent 800 covers, but it follows a very close second: 700 covers, 350 staff (including 106 chefs) and 14 telephone booking lines. Who else would be confident enough to attempt such a foolish thing but Terence Conran? Technically speaking, Mezzo is actually the restaurant in the basement, but the Mezzo empire also includes Mezzonine, the brasserie and long bar on the ground floor, and Café Mezzo next door – so get this straightened out before you attempt to make a reservation. The restaurant, brasserie and café are in turn conceived as part of a larger development which includes a residential block above, designed by CZWG Architects for the Manhattan Loft Company.

The terrazzo façade is more like an entrance to a street; vertical in emphasis, extending the full height of the elevation and jutting out at an oblique angle from the line of the street, it suggests that you 'turn the corner here'. The deep space within is surprisingly light – aided by a skylight over the front bar and reception area and a mass of downlighters beyond. But it is the double-height of the space that is all important to the success of this plan: it allows the staircase leading down to the basement to achieve a really full sweep, creates a lofty basement area, and reveals all the activities of the kitchens through a two-storey-high glazed wall. The mirrored wall on one side reflects light and movement on to both levels.

A bas relief by Allen Jones runs along the walls of Mezzo, turning into a mural on the stage sliding doors which open for jazz bands at the weekends. All furniture and fittings are designed by Terence Conran and his team in an art-deco style. The aluminium brasserie chairs, for instance, are based on a traditional American design, and the overall mood captures the essence of the 1920s in Europe and America – the Jazz Age,

**Sir Terence Conran and the CD Partnership 1995**

**the conran hegemony**

**Sir Terence Conran and the CD Partnership 1995**

## Mezzo and Mezzonine

characterised as a period of wealth, freedom and youthful exuberance. Now this image has been appropriated by our own society (driven by the pursuit of leisure, entertainment and nostalgia) as the perfect expression of a contemporary lifestyle, with Terence Conran its chief exponent.

Dining at Mezzo is all these things – a fraught, fashionable, grill-a-minute experience, with schmoochy jazz in the restaurant at night and a more frenzied dance hall atmosphere in the wee small hours of Sunday morning. Expect to see everyone, from your best friend to your dad, sipping champagne cocktails at 6pm or tucking into Beef Wellington at midnight.

ADDRESS 100 Wardour Street, London W1 (0171–314 4000)
CLIENT Conran Restaurants
SIZE Mezzo dining area 323 square metres; Mezzonine dining area 291 square metres
SEATS Mezzo: 350, Mezzonine: 300
OPEN Mezzo: Monday to Friday, 12.00–14.30; Sunday, 12.30–15.00; Monday to Thursday, 18.00–24.00 (last orders 23.30); Friday and Saturday, 18.00–0.30; Sunday, 18.00–22.30. Mezzonine: Monday to Friday, 12.00–15.00 (last orders 14.30); Saturday, 12.00–16.00 (last orders 15.30); Monday to Thursday, 17.30–23.30; Friday and Saturday, 17.30–0.30; closed Sundays
UNDERGROUND Tottenham Court Road, Leicester Square

**Sir Terence Conran and the CD Partnership 1995**

**the conran hegemony**

**Sir Terence Conran and the CD Partnership 1995**

# Bluebird

After Mezzo came Bluebird. The third of Conran's gastrodromes occupies a Grade II-listed garage and forecourt designed by Robert Sharp in 1923, when it was the largest motor garage in Europe. The original design was an eclectic mix: a utilitarian art deco frontage flanked by the formal brick of Queen Anne-revival wings, and a wall of glazed earthenware incorporating railings and lamps to mark the forecourt. The racing car motif embedded into today's Bluebird ashtrays pays homage to the original occupant. However, any other whiff of the romance of the automobile, its design, and the daredevil pursuit of high speed on land, has long been stripped from the building's carcass. Since the war it has been appropriated in turn as an ambulance station, fashion market and photography studio, with the defunct petrol pumps on the forecourt the only reminder of its original use.

It could have been the first Conran gastro-drive-thru and still had no detrimental effect on the original building or street, or the city's eating habits – who knows, it might even have enhanced them. However, Conran has the ability to identify the possibilities of combining a mixture of uses in his sites. The building was developed in two phases. Phase 1, the shell-and-core contract for the building owner, Harris & Webber, consisted of restoration and extensive repair work to the building fabric. The petrol pumps were replaced by a glass-covered fruit and vegetable stall, and the surrounding area repaved. The phase 2 fit-out by CDP encompassed the conversion of the guts of the building to suit its present use. The central two-storey garage block houses production kitchens and plant rooms in the basement, a food market on the ground floor and restaurant on the first floor. The ground floors of the flanking five-storey buildings are occupied by the Chefshop on one side (stocked with professional cooking equipment and Conran crockery) and Café Bluebird on the other, with

**CD Partnership 1997**

**Bluebird**

**the conran hegemony**

**CD Partnership 1997**

flats above. The quad creates the perfect setting for a production of *The Umbrellas of Cherbourg* – on arrival one does expect the uniformed grocers and waiters to break into a song and dance routine around the forecourt. However, it is the customers who complete the performance by posturing in formation around the aisles of exquisite produce. (On my first visit I encountered a lady in a white swimsuit and fine organza beach robe pushing a trolley full of ready-made meals, and a chap in a kilt and cap at the smoked salmon counter.)

The construction of the roof was key to the form and original use of the building. So that cars could be moved around easily, the first-floor slab was hung from the steel structure to create a column-free ground floor. The roof trusses on the first floor form a 9-metre-high central nave, adorned with kite-work by Richard Smith, and a new rooflight runs the full length of the restaurant (as at Quaglino's). On either side the ceilings are much lower, to conceal services and create a more intimate seating area overlooking the forecourt at the front and to accommodate open kitchens at the rear of the building. The car ramps which connected the basement to ground and first floors have been replaced by an elevator in the left-hand corner of the plan, tucked between café and grocery store.

The restaurant is altogether a more relaxed affair, mainly due to the quality of the space in which it is placed. The raw bar, furnishings and signature glazed banquette screens are all in place, though some items, either through over-use or over-simplified design, are beginning to lose their classic elegance and err towards corporate design.

A new staircase leads to a glass-fronted private dining room above the raw bar, and the rear block behind the kitchens has been remodelled to accommodate a private members' dining club. The reception desk integrated into the small bar near the entrance is an unfortunate penned-in

**Bluebird**

the conran hegemony

area which obscures a clear view on arrival of the length of the nave. Because of the quality and quantity of light, the restaurant is best appreciated during the daytime, when there is a more light-hearted atmosphere and a menu to address this aspect.

Conran is skilled at making places which are almost impossible to avoid and which he knows will, sooner or later, be impossible to resist. Bluebird is such a place. It not only has the allure of an unusual and beautiful building type, but it is strategically placed. Kings Road was originally a private road used by Charles II to get to Hampton Court. More recently it has been host to pierced punks and the perambulations of Chelsea Pensioners. Now it welcomes die-hard diners and convenience-foodies.

ADDRESS 350 Kings Road, London SW3 (0171–559 1000)
INTERIOR DESIGN led by Terence Conran
STRUCTURAL ENGINEER Dewhurst Macfarlane & Partners
CLIENTS Phase 1: Harris & Webber; Phase 2: Bluebird Store Limited
BUDGET £10 million for total development
SIZE 4500 square metres
SEATS 240
OPEN restaurant: Monday to Friday, 12.00–15.30; Saturday and Sunday, 11.00–16.30; Monday to Saturday, 18.00–23.00; Sunday, 18.00–22.00. Bluebird Café: Monday to Saturday, 9.00–23.00 (last orders 22.00); Sunday, 10.00–22.00 (last orders 20.30)
UNDERGROUND Sloane Square

**CD Partnership 1997**

# Zinc Bar & Grill

Going out in the West End on a Saturday night is like taking a ride to Hades. Yes, it does have its moments of pleasure, but you have to know where you are going, and in order to get there must be prepared to fight your way through a sea of cars and bodies. The best thing about the Zinc Bar is the fact that it is on Heddon Street. Until now the only thing that this small backwater (which skirts the edge of Soho but is safely over on the west side of Regent Street) has been famous for was its appearance on the cover of David Bowie's *Ziggy Stardust* album. More recently its owners, the Crown Estate, brought in architects Hawkins/Brown to upgrade the area – refurbishing and converting 40 buildings and installing new lighting and signage to give the dark back-alley new presence. From this strategic location it is possible to be in the centre of town and have the luxury of walking down the middle of the street without encountering the stench of deep-fried deep-pan pizza or an alcopop swill.

The Zinc Bar & Grill is a splinter rather than another chip off the Conran block; the idea behind Zinc is that it will become a nationwide chain to rival the likes of Café Flo, Café Rouge and the Dome. The menu and decor are a stripped-down version of those found at Quaglino's and Bluebird, with a couple of quid knocked off for lack of dazzling interior and smaller fish cakes.

The main feature in the single large space is the long zinc-covered bar along the back wall. (Bars in Paris are traditionally made of this material; hence 'zinc' is Parisian slang for bar.) The wide frontage mirrors the length of the bar and is glazed from end to end, with awnings covering pavement seating. The central dining area includes all the successfully tried and tested features: custom-made crockery, cutlery and ashtrays; Conran-designed staff and furniture, low glazed screens fixed to banquette seats; raw bar of crushed ice and fresh shellfish. All very continental and all

**Zinc Bar & Grill**

**the conran hegemony**

**CD Partnership/Terence Conran 1997**

**Zinc Bar & Grill**

available at a Conran shop near you.

So why come here at all? Because sometimes it's *nice* to eat out, you go somewhere special. But, sometimes it's *useful* and sometimes it's *essential* – and this is what Zinc is for, or could have been. However, I'm tired of always being greeted from a lectern at the door, of having to think ahead and make a reservation, or being told that I can have a table in a half empty room if I leave by 9pm. Zinc was an opportunity to redress the balance, but I was confronted with all this when dropping in for an early supper on a Saturday before going to the cinema. It is languidly formulaic, still a little on the large side, and lacks the charm and informality that it could afford with such smart and knowledgeable staff and fresh, reasonably priced food served all through the day.

ADDRESS 20 Heddon Street London W1R 7LF (0171–255 8899)
CLIENT Sir Terence Conran/Conran Restaurants
SIZE dining area 109 square metres
SEATS 116 plus extra 36 outside on terrace in summer
OPEN restaurant: Monday to Wednesday, 12.00–23.00; Thursday to Saturday, 12.00–1.00; Sunday, 12.00–18.00. Bar: Monday to Wednesday, 11.00–23.00; Thursday to Saturday, 11.00–1.00; Sunday, 12.00–18.00
UNDERGROUND Piccadilly Circus, Oxford Circus

**CD Partnership/Terence Conran 1997**

**the conran hegemony**

**CD Partnership/Terence Conran 1997**

# Le Coq d'Argent

It's amazing what a breath of French air can do for a place – 'Money Fowl' or 'Silver Chicken' don't conjure up quite the right image for a prestigious dining room commanding tremendous views of the City of London from the roof of a distinguished postmodern architectural icon. No. 1 Poultry was designed by the late Sir James Stirling and Michael Wilford on the site of the High-Victorian Mappin & Webb building. Although the new building was designed in the early 1980s it was not finished until 1998 due to a prolonged planning procedure and process of public consultation – a scheme by Mies van der Rohe was originally to have occupied the site. Stirling died before the building's completion. The plan and imagery is more 1930s cruise liner than classical villa and it is this notion which has been elaborated in Conran's nostalgic design for the restaurant.

The premises comprise the main restaurant, bar, bar terrace and restaurant garden. Inside, walnut-veneer screens and panelling, tobacco-leaf-coloured carpeting, Jura limestone flooring and banquettes upholstered in mocha-coloured velour all create the sensation of dining inside a humidor. The colours and textures of the materials used have a voluptuously muting effect on the atmosphere. All the furniture – from chairs to ashtrays – have been designed by Terence Conran specifically for Le Coq d'Argent (all but the sculpture standing on the reception desk which is by Sir Anthony Caro). Outside, the rooftop garden provides vertiginous views across London. Landscape designer Arabella Lennox-Boyd worked with James Stirling to create a formal geometric layout. The effect is mildly surreal but undermined by conservative planting.

The rooftop floor was designated on the building's plans for use as a restaurant but without a specific tenant in mind. Thus Conran's intervention is more accomplished late-1990s fit-out than harmonious period architectural feature.

**CD Partnership 1998**

CD Partnership 1998

**Le Coq d'Argent**

The most interesting aspect of the project is the means of access. The restaurant sits six floors above Bank underground station which is linked directly by elevator, then by escalator, then by the Circle and Northern lines to Waterloo, then by Eurostar to Paris Gare du Nord. In theory, a customer may travel from Paris to No. 1 Poultry without having to step outside. It beats me why any Frenchman/woman would want to make this trip to arrive in a *faux*-French restaurant in London but the idea is an elegant one.

ADDRESS No. 1 Poultry, London EC2 (0171–395 5000)
SIZE approximately 850 square metres
SEATS 399
OPEN bar: Monday to Friday, 11.30–23.30; Saturday, 18.00–23.30.
Restaurant: Monday to Friday, 11.30–15.00, 18.00–23.00 Saturday,
18.00–23.00; Sunday, 12.00–15.00, 18.30–22.30
UNDERGROUND Bank

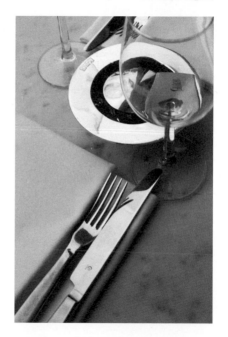

the conran hegemony

CD Partnership 1998

# modern britons

# Stephen Bull

Deep in the heart of theatreland, a small and relatively quiet restaurant has been slotted into what can only be described as someone's garage, making for a unexpectedly pleasant surprise. In the past the difficult site has been host to many a featureless, and consequently failed, restaurant. However, if anyone can make it work it is Stephen Bull – and what better foil for Stringfellow's nightclub a few doors down?

This is the third restaurant to bear Bull's neon signature over the door (crisp white to complement Stringfellow's sherbert pink), a reassuring personal guarantee that reflects his unostentatious approach and canny sensibilities. Stephen Bull embraces a modern approach to the design of his restaurants, choosing architects and designers who can create lucid architectural spaces which he can then decorate from the kitchen.

Design consultants Virgile & Stone – a team of architects, interior, furniture and graphic designers – were chosen for their previous experience in restaurant design (particularly at the Chez Gerard restaurants, see 9.2) and their ability to design or select each element of the project, from the graphic presentation of the menu to structural interventions. If this sounds alarmingly like 'a design concept' that is precisely what it is, but it has been executed with such rigour and restraint that it could quite easily have been conceived by a single, driven individual.

V & S have transformed a deep, narrow, angled plan, hostile in its three dimensions and devoid of any natural light. By using natural colours and materials and by integrating lighting into the structural surfaces, furniture and fittings, they have created a glowing, smoothly textured and intimate series of spaces. The angled, full-height glass entrance was designed to emphasise the full width and height of the otherwise unimposing frontage. The shallow entrance foyer is lined in dark timber, creating a casement through which can be seen the length of the snug bar and hints

**Virgile & Stone Associates Limited 1997**

**Stephen Bull**

**Virgile & Stone Associates Limited 1997**

**modern britons**

of the restaurant beyond. The bar is positioned at a slight angle to help integrate the two spaces visually. A simple illuminated recess in the back wall of the bar area displays spirit bottles; all other paraphernalia is stored beneath the light aspen bar. With unusually comfortable stools, it is a particularly pleasant, if compact, place to sit.

The restaurant is clearly announced by the row of tan-coloured leatherette banquette seats which are cantilevered off the right-hand wall. The high backs create a layer of upholstered wall surface and also form large sconces directing strong light up the striated concrete walls and on to the gently curved ceiling. A wall of undulating Lloyd Loom panels spanning the rear wall softens the blow of what is otherwise an abrupt termination of the room. The floor is covered with charcoal tiles. Throughout, the designers have used simple organic materials and tones in a clean, modern and original way.

Apart from an overcrowding of tables, particularly in the bar area, V & S have demonstrated that a concern for comfort and for quality in lasting materials and design can overcome the grisliest of spaces and find new life – much like Bull's own ability to make 'bread-crumbed pig's cheek and a slice of muzzle' sound appetising.

ADDRESS 12 Upper St Martin's Lane, London WC2 (0171–379 7811)
CLIENT Stephen Bull
SIZE 125 square metres
SEATS 60
OPEN Monday to Friday, 12.00–14.15, 17.45–23.30; Saturday, 17.45–23.30; closed Sunday
UNDERGROUND Leicester Square

**Virgile & Stone Associates Limited 1997**

**Virgile & Stone Associates Limited 1997**

# City Rhodes

The 'wacky' TV show really put me off. The post-punk hair-do is a bit embarrassing. However, I now completely understand why a whirlwind of excitement surrounds celebrity chef Gary Rhodes wherever he goes. Sitting face to face with one of his creations is something else. For the first time on this gastrotectonic exploration I was taken aback by what was put on the table in front of me. This is not to say that dishes elsewhere have not been exquisite, but Gary wins hands down for combining freshness, subtlety, proportion, originality, humour, and indulgence. The 'Jaffa Cake' pudding is a wonder to behold. He is absolutely true to his materials and brings out the best in them, by choosing the right cut, the right colours, the right combination. In this instance it is the food that is truly modern, far exceeding the ambitions of the environment in which it is served.

Rhodes is in fact what is now called 'executive chef' at the restaurant that bears his name. The owners, Gardner Merchant, are the second-largest contract caterers in the world and the largest in Europe, feeding everyone from football supporters to heads of state. It is therefore inevitable that a commercial glaze has been smoothed (too liberally) over this interior design.

The daring notion to appropriate the first floor of a monolithic bush-hammered concrete shell designed by Richard Seifert (of NatWest Tower and Centrepoint fame) and then to reinvent the entrance must be applauded. It is particularly interesting at night, when the horizontal band of glazing that runs the full width of the building (and restaurant) is illuminated. But, as imaginative as Gary is in the kitchen, the architect/client partnership is distinctly unimaginative in the dining room. It is hard to find in the interior the equivalent of Rhodes' confident eye for colour, scale and proportion on the plate. Walls and ceiling have been treated

**JSP Architects 1997**

with an off-white fibrous plaster which blurs the transition between surfaces and makes neat extrusions for light fittings. An assemblage of disparate details has then been placed tentatively inside: glass pavement lenses mounted in a maple bar; houndstooth-check upholstery (a nod to the conventional, suited city crowd who dine here); prints by Victor Pasmore used as ornament. The stainless-steel stair supported on two slim steel columns creates a new means of access to the restaurant and is sufficiently high tech to impress as a modern intervention.

The design approach has been to create an ordered and comfortable space which does not create anxiety, rather like a club-class lounge in an airport. The inconsistency in the overall design reflects the commercial drive behind this venture. A more idiosyncratic approach would have been not only more in tune with the host building, but an apt celebration of the talent and originality of the chef.

In 1998 Gary Rhodes opened Rhodes in the Square, a restaurant overlooking the swimming pool at the 1930s' apartment and hotel block Dolphin Square in Pimlico (London SW1).

ADDRESS 1 New Street Square, London EC4 (0171–583 1313)
CLIENT Gardner Merchant
ENGINEERS Price & Myers
BUDGET £325,000
SIZE approximately 280 square metres
SEATS 120
OPEN Monday to Friday, 12.00–14.30, 18.00–20.45
UNDERGROUND Chancery Lane, Blackfriars

**JSP Architects 1997**

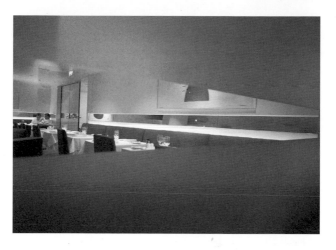

**JSP Architects 1997**

# St John

'The first essential … of architecture for pleasure is that it be serious. It must facilitate the serious business of production and consumption; and the simpler it makes that process, the better!'
*Architecture for Pleasure*, William Tatton Brown (1934)

The ultimate concoction of food, architecture and people can be found at St John. The restaurant and bar were designed by the chef … the chef was trained as an architect … architects and artists form the core of its clientele. Equipped with his diploma from the Architectural Association, Fergus Henderson set out on his career as a chef in the restaurant above the legendary French House in Soho.

The cavernous smokehouse, close to Smithfield meat market, was found by restaurateur Trevor Gulliver (of The Fire Station, Putney Bridge, see page 7.10, and PukkaBar, see page 11.10) who in turn invited Henderson and business partner Jon Spiteri (St John's *maître d'*) to take over the ground floor and basement. The building type and a strong philosophy about how to tackle the site and location drove the project.

The original structure remains almost entirely intact; a deep loading-bay entrance leads into a lofty bar area (which used to be the main smoking room) and a dining room raised above street level in the adjacent warehouse storeroom. Interior brick walls were sand-blasted throughout to remove thick black soot, then painted white; and the concrete floor was stripped back to expose the concrete aggregate and then polished. The main structural work carried out was to remove one of the walls of the largest smoke chimney in order to insert the unusually high zinc bar. The medium-sized chimney serves as the bakery and the smallest one as a store-cupboard. An internal wall separating the bar from the restaurant is punctured with high windows to allow natural light from the skylight

**Fergus Henderson 1995**

**Fergus Henderson 1995**

**modern britons**

over the bar into the deep plan of the restaurant. Factory light fittings are set out in a 2-metre grid throughout the building, suspended at the same level to create one uniform visual plane. The furniture is not beautiful, but weighty and practical; possibly the only other addition to the dining room is a Shaker coat rail which runs around the entire perimeter wall at head height.

The overall design is simple and was arrived at through an organic process (most decisions were made on site), with glimpses of the open kitchen, bakery and members of staff creating the spectacle. Few restaurants in London are as consistent in their approach and retain such integrity. The three partners display all the signs of eccentricity necessary for a long-lasting establishment: Gulliver's robust, gut-determination and humour; Spiteri's quizzical charm; and Henderson's direct, serious and instinctive approach to food and design. Get ready for seasonal staples such as cockscombs, bone marrow and pig's spleen. If your desensitised cosmopolitan palate can't cope, then have a pickled herring and a shot of schnapps, or a pint of beer and a cheese and chutney sandwich the size of a paving slab. There is a hearty epicurean culture alive here, peculiar to the northern hemisphere, and of the kind likely to be found echoing in the chambers of Mervyn Peake's Gormenghast.

ADDRESS 26 St John Street, London EC1 (0171–251 0848)
CLIENTS Trevor Gulliver, Fergus Henderson, Jon Spiteri
SIZE approximately 250 square metres
SEATS restaurant 100, bar and bakery 40
OPEN restaurant: Monday to Friday, 12.00–15.00, 18.00–23.30;
Saturday, 18.00–23.00; closed Sunday
UNDERGROUND Farringdon

**Fergus Henderson 1995**

**Fergus Henderson 1995**

# Alfred

After Fred's (the 1980s nightclub designed by Chassay Wright Architects) came Alfred, a more sober name for a more mature venture from owner Fred Taylor. The site is a traffic island between Holborn, Covent Garden and Bloomsbury. Alfred occupies the end building of a block surrounded by a generous paved area which provides the restaurant with glazed frontage on two sides.

Taylor teamed up with painter/designer/all-round-maker-of-things Quentin Reynolds to design an essentially modern British caff – with not a greasy spoon in sight. The prices are much higher than your regular roadside version (but not extortionate), and the menu and drinks list feature outstanding ingredients from all around the country (York ham, cider brandy from Somerset).

Alfred is actually a restaurant which borrows practical design elements from the traditional caff to create a simple and strictly functional interior. Formica tables, Bakelite ashtrays and standard wood and vinyl chairs have been pushed into a space/time capsule with glossy peppermint walls and menus of neon-pink Perspex. Reynold's humour, enthusiasm and intrepid eye for colour (there were no drawings or plans for this fit-out – everything was tested out on site) combined with Fred's serious understanding of his own British culture and its cultivation through his business (and his love of motorbikes) make for a well-balanced design and diet in equal measures, with neither one outwitting the other.

ADDRESS 245 Shaftesbury Avenue, London WC2 (0171–240 2566)
CLIENT Fred Taylor
BUDGET very small SEATS 60
OPEN Monday to Saturday, 12.00–15.30, 18.00–23.30 (last orders 23.30)
UNDERGROUND Tottenham Court Road

**Quentin Reynolds 1994**

**modern britons**

**Quentin Reynolds 1994**

# R K Stanley's

R K Stanley's is located directly north of Soho, in an area long associated with the rag trade rather than the cutting edge of the restaurant industry. That is, until very recently when suddenly, within the space of about six months, three high-profile restaurants are opening in the area and hotelier Ian Schrager with architect Philippe Starck (of Royalton and Paramount Hotel fame in New York) is converting the former Sanderson wallpaper showrooms on Newman Street into a hotel.

Camden Borough Council's planning policy in the area has been to try to preserve the showroom usage on premises which come up for lease or sale, in order to maintain a dense business district, with restaurants confined to particular streets such as Great Titchfield Street.

R K Stanley's is one of the first to break the mould, in more ways than one. This particular building was not hindered by a showroom frontage. With heavy timber doors and an understated inlaid sign, it looks more like a club, reminiscent of London's old chop houses where frontages were obscured with stained glass and heavy curtains, for privacy and warmth respectively. The comparisons do not end here. The restaurant redefines the consumption of hearty food and good beer. The interior comprises a central, narrow, U-shaped timber bar, backed by a crisp stainless-steel wall of draught beer pumps, and an open kitchen at the back of the space serving bangers (freshly made on the premises) and mash.

All but one of the windowless walls are lined with an exaggerated tongue-and-groove panelling, painted a pale marrowfat pea green. The remaining long wall is lined with large tiles made of reconstituted Portland stone (a form of concrete). The geometric relief pattern impressed into the tiles is a copy of one of Frank Lloyd Wright's designs which illustrate his notion that 'concrete is a plastic material – susceptible to the imagination'.

**Quentin Reynolds 1997**

**Quentin Reynolds 1997**

## R K Stanley's

The furniture, all designed and tested on site specifically for the restaurant, is fixed to a pink terrazzo floor. From swivelling armchair bar stools to ash and red-leatherette banquettes, the shapes and proportions combine the satisfying comfort of a 1950s American diner seat with the simple practicality of a 17th-century ale-house bench.

That national staple the sausage – in all its forms, from black pudding to a Glamorgan – has never truly gone out of fashion (though it has acquired a health warning). R K Stanley's has taken the democratic decision to revive the sausage as a wholesome and inexpensive way both to attract newcomers and to satisfy the foodiest of foodie appetites. The design of the premises stimulates our increasingly discerning sensory palate with hand-picked elements, devices, materials and dimensions, all of which are branded with a traditional seal of approval but adapted to specific requirements and modern expectations.

The name of the restaurant is a figment of the imaginations of owner Fred Taylor and designer Quentin Reynolds, created specifically to be fashionably non-fashionable and to reflect the stalwart quality of their venture: Stanley Matthews ... Stanley Bowles ... Stanley Kubrick ... Stanley Spencer ...

ADDRESS 6 Little Portland Street, London W1 (0171–462 0099)
CLIENT Fred Taylor
BUDGET approximately £1600 per square metre
SIZE ground floor and basement approximately 400 square metres
SEATS 145
OPEN Monday to Saturday, 12.00–15.30, 18.00–23.30
UNDERGROUND Oxford Circus

**Quentin Reynolds 1997**

**Quentin Reynolds 1997**

# Coast

Coast is the result of a youthful collaboration between chef Stephen Terry, Australian designer Marc Newson, Savile Row tailor Richard James, Grace Architecture, and entrepreneur Oliver Peyton of Atlantic Bar & Grill renown (see 5.2).

The entire concept, from the menu through·to furniture, is feverishly futuristic – a sort of cosmo(politan) sci-fi adventure. The site was an old Volvo showroom featuring a full-height, full-width front window (the type that tempts you to drive through it at high speed). It now serves as a people showroom. The restaurant is located on the ground floor, which is cut away at the back to reveal more seating in the basement below. The entire space has been treated with a seamless surface which blends away all the corners in the room, creating pimples around light fittings and a voluptuously organic spiral stairwell to connect the two floors. The Quatermass quality of this surface contrasts with highly crafted features such as the parquet floor.

Chairs and bar stools are made of wood inlaid with yellow Formica. The design by Newson refers both to the utilitarianism of a piece of school furniture and to the casual formality of a lounge suit – well made and essentially timeless. The bar stools are particularly comfortable, which makes a pleasant change. The bathrooms are a triumph – a long corridor lined in small round mosaic tiling is supremely hygienic, and large brushed stainless-steel fittings from France are absolutely functional.

Coast has had very mixed reviews in the past, primarily criticising it for its unforgivingly modern interior, spiky staff and, worst of all, the desolate basement seating (perhaps it is the spring in the step of the spiral stair which makes critics queasy). I can confidently say that my experience of dining here was one of the best and most modern I have had in London. One thing that critics have found hard to knock is the chef's

**Grace Architecture with designer Marc Newson 1995**

**Grace Architecture with designer Marc Newson 1995**

talent. After perfect dry martinis at the discreet bar on the ground floor, we sampled adventurously eclectic combinations of flavours and textures from the menu.

A gesture to the social science of eating out is the installation by artist Angela Bulloch (1997 Turner Prize nominee) called 'Luna Cosine Machine'. The drawing machine moves to the sound and movement of people in the room and plots lines directly on to a wipe-clean wall surface, producing a picture or graph each day. The seismic readings are linked to the till system so that your bill contains a print-out of the picture that has been created over the course of your visit.

ADDRESS 26B Albemarle Street, London W1 (0171–495 5999)
CLIENT Oliver Peyton
SIZE 185 square metres
SEATS 140
OPEN 12.00–15.00 (last orders 14.45), 18.00–24.00 (last orders 23.45)
UNDERGROUND Green Park

**Grace Architecture with designer Marc Newson 1995**

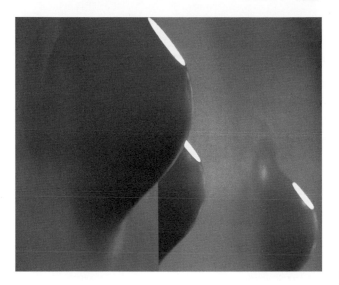

**Grace Architecture with designer Marc Newson 1995**

# Quo Vadis

Formerly the classic Italian restaurant in Soho, Quo Vadis reopened in 1997 amid ferocious publicity. The professional team was centred around a celebrity collaboration between chef Marco Pierre White and artist Damien Hirst (the violent consequences of this partnership seem unimaginable), with restaurateur Jimmy Lahoud of The Criterion and L'Escargot, Jonathan Kennedy (previously of the Groucho Club), and Matthew Freud of Freud Communications. Time was of the essence for such an ambitious project: there could be no delay in getting the doors open. Right up to the opening night builders were falling over each other to complete the work on time.

Had it not been for the intervention of Long & Kentish (architects of The Ivy refurbishment; see 1.6) one wonders if the end result might not have been entirely disastrous. Instead the refurbishment is simply unfortunate. The architects were brought in at the last minute to retain the atmosphere of the traditional restaurant on the ground floor, and to work with Damien Hirst to create a 'younger' bar on the first floor. The brief was to create an image which would have maximum effect with the minimum of effort, the priority being to organise the restaurant space.

The long, thin horizontal footprint of the new restaurant fills the shoes of the previous one; a series of rooms spans four bays of Dean Street, the original stained-glass frontage stretching the full width of the site with the entrance at one end. The rooms have been opened out to create a lighter and more unified plan. Adornment takes the form of the hanging of a large collection of contemporary art works – a collection which is so wholeheartedly tasteful that one suspects it was bought as a job lot. The existing chairs have been reupholstered in pale grey leather – a similar shade to the seared tuna on my plate. Asparagus was limp, unlike the excessively perky downlighting throughout the restaurant. Ledges

**Long & Kentish 1997**

## Quo Vadis

between banquette seats serve as plinths for small sculptures and loitering waiters.

The upstairs bar doubles as a small gallery for work by Damien Hirst, Sarah Lucas and friends. Hip young chicks sipping cocktails next to a cow's skull with rotting flesh attached provided journalists and photographers with a neat topical contrast, and liberal emotions were shaken and stirred. The bar itself, although touched by Hirst's own hand – a spot painting on mirror forms the central panel – is distinctly undistinguished and suffers a fate as unconvincing as the restaurant below.

It is apparent through the patchwork that Quo Vadis is mutton dressed as lamb. This disappointment can only be due to the fact that the venture was not given adequate time to be designed to the level of detail that such a very special site and dynamic idea deserve.

ADDRESS 26–29 Dean Street, London W1 (0171–437 9585)
CURATOR Damien Hirst
CLIENTS Marco Pierre White, Jonathan Kennedy, Matthew Freud, Jimmy Lahoud
SIZE 800 square metres on four floors
SEATS 92
OPEN Monday to Friday, 12.00–15.00, 18.00–23.30; Saturday and Sunday, 18.00–23.30
UNDERGROUND Tottenham Court Road

**Long & Kentish 1997**

**Quo Vadis**

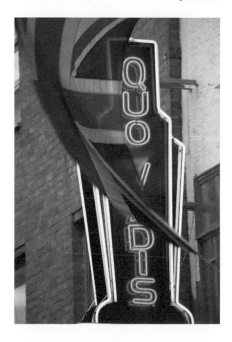

**modern britons**

**Long & Kentish 1997**

# Pharmacy Restaurant and Bar

In Gordon Burn's introduction to artist Damien Hirst's autobiographical work *I Want to Spend the Rest of My Life Everywhere, with Everyone, One to One, Always, Forever, Now* (Booth-Clibborn Editions 1997), he outlines Walter Benjamin's view that 'while artistic experiments are rejected by the masses as "incomprehensible" when encountered as part of avant-garde art, they are accepted and appreciated when seen as part of mass culture'. Hirst has made his work available in every format, from spot paintings and dissected cow-in-tank sculptures to music videos and t-shirts. This is not to say that they are not all rigorously sculptural in their integrity – as he has said, 'it's all art to me'. For one whose overriding obsession is with 'the nearness and inevitability of death' but whose fundamental statement about his position is 'Art seems to me to be about life', what better medium to be using now but the environment of a restaurant?

The prominent site has long been inhabited by restaurants but has had a fairly ropy history. For many years it was Cleopatra, home of plate-smashing Greek cuisine; in 1996 it became Cento 50 which *Time Out* described as having 'fashionable aspirations'. Sadly these aspirations only lasted 15 months.

Jonathan Kennedy, Matthew Freud and Damien Hirst had worked together at Quo Vadis (see page 3.24), but under less satisfactory circumstances – there Hirst's input was more that of a curator than artist and designer of the space. At Pharmacy the balance of roles has been readdressed – Hirst has had free reign to design the premises as an art work accommodating a bar on the ground floor and a restaurant on the first.

The nature of the existing building lends itself perfectly to the generic name and Hirst's earlier tank and cabinet works; the crisp white-rendered front elevation frames vast horizontal picture windows on both floors either side of a central glazed entrance. The ground-floor windows wrap

**Mike Rundell/Damien Hirst 1998**

Pharmacy Restaurant and Bar

modern britons

**Mike Rundell/Damien Hirst 1998**

**Pharmacy Restaurant and Bar**

around the sides of the building and display Hirst's medicine and pharmaceutical instrument works (arranged as a model of the body, those at the top relating to the head, and so on) and a photographic piece positioned in the entrance to form the back of the centrally located bar. The restaurant upstairs is dominated by the spot-painting series with spot wallpaper and spot windows. A glass wall screen forms a corridor between the staircase, kitchens, bathrooms and the dining room, creating a casement in which to display the diners. Graph-paper tiles in the bathrooms are also by Hirst. Chairs and banquette seats are by Jasper Morrison. Uniforms by Prada. The subtitle 'restaurant and bar' on the frontage replaces the original green neon cross sign (associated with all continental pharmacies) which unfortunately led to too many incidents of mistaken identity … old folk handing their prescriptions over the bar, that sort of thing.

There is an established tradition of artists making work for restaurants and artists opening restaurants themselves (for example, Gordon Matta-Clark made Food in New York during the 1970s). The manner in which we eat and drink is unlikely to be revolutionised at Pharmacy (there is an experienced and competent team of chefs and restaurateurs behind the project), but our expectations of the way in which we experience works of art has been redefined.

ADDRESS 150 Notting Hill Gate, London W11 (0171–221 2442)
CLIENTS Liam Carson, Damien Hirst, Matthew Freud, Jonathan Kennedy
SIZE 300 square metres SEATS 110 in upstairs restaurant
OPEN bar: Monday to Saturday, 12.00–15.00, 18.00–1.00 Friday and Saturday –2.00); Sunday, 11.15–15.00, 18.00–22.30. Restaurant: Monday to Saturday, 12.30–15.00, 19.00–0.00; Sunday, 12.30–15.00, 19.00–22.30
UNDERGROUND Notting Hill Gate, Holland Park

**Mike Rundell/Damien Hirst 1998**

**modern britons**

**Mike Rundell/Damien Hirst 1998**

# Circus

Fay Maschler, the *grande dame* of food criticism, asked a question two years ago when former City financier Christopher Bodker organised a team of 70 investors to set up his first restaurant, The Avenue (see 4.12). The same question is still being asked: 'Can a group of investors with experience in the City rather than catering set up and run a successful restaurant by packaging it correctly?' By all accounts, The Avenue is perceived as a success (it is usually packed out), and Bodker has since become a full-time restaurateur, which must give some indication of his commitment to his cause. Furthermore, he has opened a second venture here at Circus.

The site is the former Granada Television Studios off Golden Square. The restaurant occupies the ground floor. The space is naturally lit on three sides through large steel windows which are screened from the pavement by 'boxes of light' made from two screens of fine translucent voile. The quality of light that emanates from the screens is of the most penetratingly white variety. Service facilities are conspicuous by their absence; all the necessary ones are contained in illuminated glass boxes constructed of glass sandwich panels, silkscreened with translucent colours before being laminated. Regimental rows of square tables, draped in starched white cloths, stand on a wenge timber floor. The chairs, also designed by Chipperfield, have a generous plasticity of form and are upholstered in a mushroom-coloured suede – a curtsy in the strictly taciturn setting of the restaurant interior.

The cocktail bar in the basement is split over two levels. A U-shaped bar overlooks the seating area below and the Zen landscaping of a small courtyard. Larger ottomans and tables on this lower level are reflected in the black vitrolite glass and mirrors which line the long wall opposite the courtyard.

**David Chipperfield Architects 1997**

**David Chipperfield Architects 1997**

**Circus**

This ain't no big top. There are no lions holding their tamer's heads delicately in their jaws and David Chipperfield has not been spotted on site in red tailcoat and top hat and collarless shirt – it is altogether a very sober affair.

ADDRESS 1 Upper St James Street, London W1 (0171–534 4000)
STRUCTURAL ENGINEER Dewhurst Macfarlane & Partners
CLIENT Mirror Image Restaurants plc
SIZE bar and restaurant 460 square metres
SEATS 130
OPEN Monday to Friday, 12.00–15.00 (–16.00 Saturday); Monday to Thursday, 17.45–24.00 (–00.30 Friday and Saturday)
UNDERGROUND Piccadilly Circus

**David Chipperfield Architects 1997**

**David Chipperfield Architects 1997**

# Titanic

The site was previously occupied by The Original Carvery Restaurant of the Regent Palace Hotel. This opened in 1959 as the first carvery restaurant in the world as devised by J D Salmon who had picked up the idea on visiting friends in a farmhouse in Dorset where guests were encouraged to carve their own meat. The Carvery's art-deco interior was in fact based on the *Queen Mary* ocean liner. The romance associated with this style has recently seen a resurgence. An anthropologist might say it is because of a naive nostalgia for a carefree era. A cynic would suggest that Hollywood has had such a profound effect on our lives that we no longer need or want to make the distinction between the screen and real life. At Titanic both are truths for while skimming through The White Star Line menu (aiming to please everyone and astounding no one; from pea and ham soup and liver and bacon to terryaki salmon and bang bang chicken) there is every chance of bumping into any number of minor and major stars sipping cocktails in the bar.

The interior has been 'refreshed' by the same designers who worked on Quaglino's, which may explain why the organisational aspects of the space seem familiar. The descent through large revolving doors into a vast dining room induces a swagger in the most apprehensive guest. The room is dominated by a vast glitterball suspended over the central bar which comes into its own when the dance floor behind gets into full swing in the evenings. A new uniformly cream terrazzo floor spreads out beneath tables and chocolate-coloured chairs (see page 2.8) which are arranged to the left and right behind timber and etched-glass screens. Details are retained and enhanced; all the existing stained rosewood timber has been reconditioned to capture the spirit of the age. New elements such as the cloakroom kiosk have been laminated in the same dark wood. The existing panelling featured smoky mirrors which are now interspersed

**United Designers 1998**

**United Designers 1998**

with panels of gold leaf to increase 'the glow'. Scalloped ceiling coffers painted light blue and holding frosted-glass shades cast a calm even light during the day, while at night a sultry incandescence is exuded from wall sconces integrated into the panelling.

Opening in the same hotel block as the Atlantic Bar & Grill (see page 5.2) caused a furore. Allegedly, Oliver Peyton had made an agreement with the owners of the hotel, Trust House Forte, that a similar venture would not be permitted to open on the premises, but when Forte sold out to Granada (key shareholders in Marco Pierre White, Criterion plc), obvious conflicts of interest arose. However, the deal has spawned a thousand puns and no doubt both venues have benefited from the publicity. The name therefore is more accurately a reference to the adjective which describes the physical and behavioural proportions of its chef/owner than a faithful reconstruction of the jinxed ocean liner or the birth of a new line in themed restaurants based on Great Disasters of the World.

ADDRESS 81 Brewer Street, London W1 (0171-437 1912)
CLIENTS Marco Pierre White, Criterion plc
SEATS approximately 220
OPEN restaurant: Monday to Saturday, 12.00–14.30, 17.30–2.30; Sunday, 17.30–23.00. Bar: Monday to Saturday, 12.00–14.30, 17.30–2.30; Sunday, 17.30–22.30
UNDERGROUND Piccadilly Circus

**United Designers 1998**

**United Designers 1998**

# mega sites

# The Criterion

The Criterion was designed by Thomas Verity (architect of the old Empire in Leicester Square and the Comedy Theatre, Panton Street). The architect beat 15 others in a competition held by the railway caterers, Spiers & Pond. Verity's proposal included a theatre, restaurants and banqueting rooms. The budget was £25,000 but by the time it was completed in 1874 the final cost was nearer £80,000. The plan included The Long Bar on the ground floor and a basement concert hall. The latter soon became the Criterion Theatre (one of the first theatres to be built entirely underground), and the ground floor was extended in 1878 and 1885 to include large function rooms.

At the time the Long Bar was also known as the Marble Hall. The Byzantine splendour of its gilded mosaic ceiling lit by bunches of tulip-shaped candelabra, and the marble-lined walls embedded with semi-precious mosaics (malachite, turquoise, rose quartz, mother-of-pearl, lapis-lazuli), still exist today, creating the most spectacularly enchanting dining room in London. The ceiling alone would cost £1.25 million to install today.

The period when The Criterion was built was marked by a Victorian exuberance for collecting and an eclectic mix of neo-styles. It is therefore no surprise that Verity should combine a façade of Portland Stone in the style of the French Renaissance with the most exotic of decorative arts to adorn the interior of his temple of delight. The plan of the Marble Hall is based on a series of domed squares (a Near-Eastern Byzantine church form), and beyond three arches at the back it is raised to create a smoking divan. The whole room measures 45 metres long but is only 7 metres wide.

Spiers & Pond went bankrupt in 1917. Since then the restaurant has been repeatedly redefined to keep up with the times. It was first of all taken over by Buzzards, who initiated the Criterion Orchestra and tea and

**David Collins 1995**

dinner dances. During the war, the banqueting rooms above were used by the BBC. Having long since lost the bar, Charles Forte reopened the premises as The Puritan Maid cafeteria in 1949 and it established a reputation as the fastest cafeteria in the world. It could serve 16–20 people a minute due to three innovations: each customer was handed two sets of cutlery wrapped in a napkin; tea and coffee were served at the table; and customers paid on leaving. A major part of the attraction was the 5-metre-long Minimax gold-plated coffee-machine. In 1960 the Marble Hall turned into the Grill-and-Griddle, where customers sat at a counter directly opposite the chefs; the marble walls were lined with Formica to protect them from cooking fumes. By 1975 the kitchen had been removed from the hall, which briefly became a Quality Inn.

The Marble Hall was restored to its former glory by Trusthouse Forte when it opened the Criterion Brasserie in 1984. Richard Daniels of Bell Daniels Slater Partnership was responsible for removing the Formica (which had successfully preserved the marble) and cleaning all the surfaces with an acid-based solution to bring out the natural colours. The terrazzo floor was so damaged that it was replaced with beige, black and terracotta mosaic. For ten years the brasserie was given a 1920s slant – it was open all day, a bar was reinstated and the room scattered with bentwood and cane chairs and wooden tables. This informality in such splendid surroundings was, for me, the great attraction of the Criterion – and it was accessible to just about anyone.

By now Grade I-listed, Verity's building was always destined for better things. Under the new management of Marco-Pierre White (the chef with rock-star status) and Forte plc, it reopened in 1995 as The Criterion. The skill of David Collins, architect of many high-profile restaurants in London hotels, lies in attending to detail and in working with craftsmen

**David Collins 1995**

**David Collins 1995**

to create bespoke fixtures and furniture for lasting interiors. At The Criterion he emphasises the Byzantine influences of the original decor, inspired by his research into Indian, Turkish, Byzantine and Ottoman styles. Original features remain untouched but are enhanced by a new range of finishes, fabrics, furniture and lighting. There are two sets of chairs: the restaurant chair has a black lacquer frame with maroon leather upholstery, the bar chair is of ebonised wood with a stud motif. Banquette seats are covered in patterned velvet. A more intimate light level is created along the walls at head height with lantern lights draped in upturned ogee-shaped silk shades. Elsewhere, cast-bronze bamboo lamp bases with beaded and corded shades strike a more modern pose.

Spiers & Pond's entrepreneurial flair and the beauty of Verity's interior cannot be surpassed, and have endured through all its shapes and forms and occupants. However, it has to be said that the voracious tactics of the current restaurant management more than detract from the occasion. However fabulous the food, moving diners into the bar for their dessert (to make way for a new sitting) and bullish and combative service is no way to treat eager customers who seem more than willing to part with their gold cards. Such tactics smart like raw onion in the eyes.

ADDRESS 224 Piccadilly, London W1 (0171-930 0488)
CLIENTS (at time of design) Marco Pierre White, Sir Rocco Forte; currently owned by MPW
BUDGET £500,000
SIZE 315 square metres (dining room only) SEATS 195
OPEN Monday to Saturday, 12.00–14.30, 18.00–24.00; Sunday, 12.00–16.00, 18.00–22.30
UNDERGROUND Piccadilly

**David Collins 1995**

**David Collins 1995**

# Bank

Julyan Wickham is well versed in the design of restaurants, particularly high-profile ones. Architect of the devastatingly cool Zanzibar in the 1970s (no longer in existence), he went on in the mid 1980s to design Le Champenois in the City and, more importantly, Kensington Place (see page 1.24). This marked a turning point for restaurant design and subsequently led to the 5th Floor at Harvey Nichols (page 6.2). Bank is a response to the current mania for mega-restaurants (those seating at least 200 people). The project is Wickham's most lavish to date.

The restaurant and bar are located on the ground floor and basement of a steel-framed 1914 building once occupied (surprisingly enough) by a bank. The site stretches from the crescent of Aldwych at the front through to Kean Street at the back. Presented with an old high-ceilinged banking hall with a deep and irregular plan, the architect has had to take a fresh approach to the organisation of functions in order to make efficient and dramatic use of the space.

The starting point, and crux, of the plan, was the insertion of a linear kitchen (the largest single unit ever made) into the narrower, middle section of the space. It connects the U-shaped bar at the front with the serving station at the rear and faces directly on to the dining room. This kitchen, used for the final theatrical preparation of dishes which have come up from a more substantial kitchen below, is screened by a glass wall which forms a processional route from bar to restaurant. Kean Street is at a higher level than the dining-room floor, so to avoid potentially embarrassing worm's-eye views of passers-by and yet maintain this major source of natural light, deep fins have been added to the window openings. Projecting into the restaurant they act as a kind of *brise-soleil*.

Every detail has been addressed to create an exuberant yet harmonious and rigorous design which is ultimately for the customer's entertainment.

**Wickham & Associates Architects 1997**

**Wickham & Associates Architects 1997**

## Bank

The custom-made furniture (chairs, bar stools and waiters' stations) made up of modernist spheres, padded crescents and stained, wooden cut-outs are now distinctive as Wickham signature pieces. However, the feature that overwhelmingly unifies the whole space is the chandelier. Industrial in scale, it weighs 26 tons and contains 3629 pieces of glass. The icy green edges of each sliver create a watery pool which stands out against the hot red and yellow walls and furnishings. The invisibly illuminated mass changes in depth, texture and colour as you walk beneath it – inspiring awe and peril. It is a truly beautiful object. In complete contrast, but again a consistent feature in all Wickham's restaurants, are the two large murals, by his daughter Pola. Their subject matter, a deserted Coney Island, suggests a sentimental yearning for the slightly seedy side of popular amusements of the past and provides an antidote to the extravagance and high gloss of this contemporary playground.

Bank's proximity to the many hotels and theatres in the area means that the day starts with breakfasts and continues through to after-theatre dinners. Yes, it is seriously noisy, particularly at night, but then the restaurant does seat 220 and each and every guest is there to have a good time.

ADDRESS 1 Kingsway, London WC2 (0171–379 9797)
CLIENT Marchthistle (Tony Allen and Ron Truss)
STRUCTURAL ENGINEER Dewhurst Macfarlane & Partners
BUDGET £1.8 million
SIZE approximately 1000 square metres
SEATS 230
OPEN Monday to Saturday, 07.00–11.30, 12.00–14.45, 17.30–23.00;
Sunday, 12.00–14.45, 17.30–22.30
UNDERGROUND Temple, Aldwych, Holborn

**Wickham & Associates Architects 1997**

**Wickham & Associates Architects 1997**

# The Avenue

The night I visited The Avenue it was absolutely packed, to the extent that people from the bar were overflowing into the restaurant and customers sitting at 'table one' found themselves joined by several uninvited guests. Our table was booked for 9pm, but an hour and a few drinks later – and still without a table – we clung to our self-respect and left.

An off-peak visit reveals a restaurant and bar inserted into a 1920s banking hall. The new use has inherited and welcomed many of the attributes of the original building type, such as a very deep plan and high ceilings, but another feature, the entrance, has been removed and filled with two pieces of full-height frameless glass – a Mather signature piece.

Here Mather has broken out of his more familiar Zen mould, but still indulges in his enjoyment of fluid space. The interior has been stripped back and simply plastered, leaving natural and artificial light to articulate the space. Original rooflights were revealed and reglazed with frameless panels, and the back window opened up to expose neighbouring buildings. The bar itself (another contender for the longest bar in London) gives off a warm glow from its yellow, laminated-glass top. Spanish limestone floors and sensible American cherrywood furniture are the gentlest of details in a generally gutsy and glamorous space. Mather has undoubtedly achieved the New York feel that the client asked for.

ADDRESS 7–9 St James Street, London SW1 (0171–321 2111)
ENGINEER Dewhurst Macfarlane & Partners
CLIENT Christopher Bodker (on behalf of 70 shareholders)
SIZE approximately 230 square metres in total SEATS 180
OPEN Monday to Thursday, 12.00–15.00, 18.00–24.00; Friday and Saturday, 12.00–15.00, 18.00–00.30; Sunday, 12.00–16.00, 19.00–22.30
UNDERGROUND Green Park

**Rick Mather Architects 1996**

mega sites

**Rick Mather Architects 1996**

# La Belle Epoque

It is like eating inside a Chanel handbag. It is what Terence Conran might do if he wasn't so downright tasteful. It is what the Parisians do really well – naturally.

La Belle Epoque is an evocative description for a period in French cultural life that occurred in the late 19th century. It embraced good living and innovation in the decorative arts and was expressed in the art nouveau style and in the art of Lautrec and Mucha. In Britain the era was known as the Naughty Nineties, a 'golden age'. Since then, Britain as a nation has persuaded itself to feel deeply embarrassed by its lack of cultural sophistication compared to the rest of Europe, particularly when it comes to food and the serving of it. We are mocked for it but also seem to take wry pleasure in condoning a lacklustre attitude. The 1980s and 1990s have been all about positively re-educating us to be more aesthetically restrained; to be more continental in our habits; to appreciate how natural colours, materials and ingredients can be contemporary too; and to adopt a roving eclecticism as befits the most accomplished of cosmopolitan citizens.

This is where La Belle Epoque comes in. It is the largest restaurant complex in Europe, seating a total of 800 people. La Brasserie on the ground floor spills out on to the pavement, bordered by clipped hedges. La Salle, the largest of the three restaurants, occupies the main body of the ground floor and is defined by an avenue of palm trees and windows looking on to a team of 30 chefs working away in the kitchen. Le Bar and L'Oriental (the flagship restaurant of La Belle Epoque) lie seductively in the basement. They are both open in the evening only, and seat 160 people in opulent surroundings: *objets d'art* are set against mahogany surfaces and reflected in bevelled mirrors, tables are laid with cream and black linen and china designed by Versace.

**Jonathan Dunn Associates 1997**

**Jonathan Dunn Associates 1997**

## La Belle Epoque

La Belle Epoque has sunk its highly polished fingernails into the sun-dried flesh of London's restaurant scene. No expense has been spared: it glistens from top to toe in every highly polished glass, brass or granite surface, just like a restaurant on the Champs Elysées. Everything, from corporate identities, menus, crockery and packaging to door furniture, has been specially designed to the highest specification. Every waiter is starched and pressed flat, and the food is scrubbed so clean you could eat off it. Columns are adorned with addorsed figures. The ecstatic expressions on their faces mimic those on the faces of the customers who gaze in wonder at the chocolate-box array of groceries in the Emporium, which forms a prelude to the entrance.

A slice of metropolitan Paris has come to London, and Londoners have taken to it like ducks *à l'orange*.

ADDRESS 151 Draycott Avenue, London SW3 (0171–460 5000)
DESIGN CONSULTANTS Pocknell Studio
CLIENT La Belle Epoque
SIZE entire building approximately 10,000 square metres
SEATS 750
OPEN La Brasserie: 8.00–24.00 (–23.00 Sunday). La Salle: 12.00–15.30,
17.30–24.00 (–23.00 Sunday). L'Oriental: Monday to Saturday,
17.30–1.00
UNDERGROUND South Kensington

**Jonathan Dunn Associates 1997**

**Jonathan Dunn Associates 1997**

# Mash

Mash is the southern offspring of Mash & Air in Manchester, a specially designed micro-brewery with bar and restaurant attached. Both places are high in underlying concept, i.e. that the brewery be visible and an integral part of the design. The hyper-modern world of abstraction and extrusion of shape and space is rapidly becoming a house style for Peyton's restaurant ventures (compare Coast, page 3.20). Soft architecture is pursued throughout the interior from absorbent wall textures to padded furniture (one becoming indistinguishable from the other) with many one-off items specially commissioned for the restaurant such as the humidor by Bill Amberg and staff footwear by Hush Puppies. Curves are a consistent detail throughout, used where any one plane meets another, and surfaces and edges are rounded off to create the impression of a seamless environment. A curved tubular space has been inserted into an existing shell to contain all working parts on two floors – deli, bar, brewery, conversation pit, cloakroom, kitchens – leaving the central spaces free for tables. Cut-out openings reveal the functions.

The treatment of the stairwell connecting ground and first floors achieves the ultimate in plasticity. The pebbledash/epoxy coating on walls and floor creates malleable soffits for fixtures and fittings and has astoundingly absorbent acoustic properties, creating a spongy intestinal space. It is just unfortunate that the material is confined to the stairs. Noise is the most profound problem in most restaurants today. Given the trend for converting large sites, it is surprising how few designers and architects address this issue.

Specially commissioned artworks are a significant feature at Mash: a sensor in the front door activates changing messages on 'The Love Machine' by 'Gorgeous' Murray Partridge, a lightbox work by American artist John Currin adorns the walls of the sunken bar lounge, and over-

**mega sites**

**FIN Architects 1998**

## Mash

seeing the entrance is a brushed aluminium figure by Don Brown.

Mash could be described as more of a food factory than a mere restaurant. The menu is a reflection of this shift in scale – it is painful to peruse (pizza chips, confit of duck pizza) and difficult to digest. The hierarchy of dining areas is also unfounded: although prices increase from downstairs bar to first-floor restaurant, there is little to differentiate the quality of space and atmosphere. Visiting Mash is a lifestyle choice, not a culinary one and therefore a 1990s sloganised description is appropriate: here high-street fashion meets fad food.

ADDRESS 19–21 Great Portland Street, London W1 (0171–637 5555)
CLIENT Oliver Peyton
SIZE 1100 square metres
SEATS 400
OPEN Monday to Friday, 8.00–15.00 (breakfast until 12.00),
18.00–1.00; Saturday and Sunday, 11.00–16.30 (brunch), 18.00–1.00
UNDERGROUND Oxford Circus

**FIN Architects 1998**

**FIN Architects 1998**

# Che

A case of context not content describes this restaurant, bar and cigar lounge that attracts the kind of clientele that have cashmere complexions and sweat *eau de cologne*. Entrepreneur Hani Farsi has indulged his passion for art, wine and cigars – but not necessarily in that order. The premises is another bank conversion (a recurring theme in recent restaurant design) but this was no ordinary bank. Che occupies the basement, ground and first floors of the shorter of two Grade II-listed towers designed for The Economist by Alison and Peter Smithson in 1964. The pair of buildings and their surrounding raised plaza are an outstanding architectural specimen demonstrating that planning the spaces around buildings is as vital to the dynamic of the city as the buildings themselves.

Fletcher Priest have dutifully referred to original plans held in the RIBA's drawings collection and to Peter Smithson to 'inform' their interior design (the façades remain untouched). The escalators and central service core have been retained as a dramatic means of ascent to the restaurant on the first floor with views on arrival on to the plaza and twin tower beyond. The lofty proportions of this floor and the inconceivably large expanse of each window frame, which make up 360 degrees of glazed perimeter wall, leave diners like dead leaves at the bottom of an empty swimming pool. The stretched-fabric ceiling light is inspired by the original lighting detail. The bar is on the ground floor to the left of the lobby entrance with the cigar lounge beyond. The layering of new surfaces and the finishes in these areas, designed to create a new 'look', do not belong to the school of architectural thought which created this piece of modern city in the 1960s.

Farsi's passions: he owns an extraordinary collection of photographs of Che Guevara taken by Korda, the Santos Brothers and Che's own personal bodyguard Perfecto Romero Ramirez. The pictures will be

**Fletcher Priest 1998**

**Fletcher Priest 1998**

exhibited one at a time in the cigar lounge and it will take more than nine years to view the entire collection. Other work is described as being 'inspired by the Pop Art Movement', suggesting that it does not actually include any original pieces from this period (also an accurate description of the menu). Wine: well, the sommelier has an impeccable pedigree and has created not one but two wine lists which alone would fill this book. And the cigars … although on wall-to-wall display, what sounds like an outstanding collection (including 20 types of pre-Castro and pre-embargo cigars, Havanas from the 1960s and '70s) is strangely confined to a very small area of the site.

You may (and should) read this in disbelief. We may no longer be astonished when millionaire pop stars speak out for the cancellation of third-world debt, but to set up a restaurant capitalising on the name of an awesome revolutionary (executed for his cause) in conjunction with the colonic irrigation of this fine building is verging on the tasteless.

ADDRESS 23 St James Street, London SW1 (0171–747 9380)
CLIENT Hani Farsi
SIZE 7500 square metres
SEATS 210 (restaurant/bar/cigar lounge)
OPEN restaurant: Monday to Friday, 12.00–15.00, 17.30–23.30; Saturday, 17.30–23.30. Bar: Monday to Friday, 11.00–23.00; Saturday, 17.30–23.00
UNDERGROUND Piccadilly Circus

**Fletcher Priest 1998**

Fletcher Priest 1998

# hotel restaurants

# Atlantic Bar & Grill

The Atlantic Bar & Grill is probably the most decadent drinking establishment in London. Opened in 1994, it was the first of the large bar/restaurants and is reputed to serve more champagne than any other establishment in Europe. The unique appeal of the Atlantic was, and still is, its seductive decor, which even manages to bring the romance back into bad behaviour and throwing-up after having had one too many.

The Atlantic was the inspired idea of Oliver Peyton, who has since gone on to create Coast (see page 3.20), Mash & Air in Manchester and Mash (see page 4.18). He discovered the site in the basement of the Regent Palace Hotel, built at the height of the ocean liner era between 1912 and 1915 by Sir Henry Tanner (who subsequently redesigned Oxford Circus), F J Willis and W J Ancell. By the 1960s the passion for art deco – and basement cocktail bars – had faded, and Peyton persuaded the hotel's owners, Trust House Forte, to lease out what had become a sorry heap of disused conference rooms. With the help of designer David Connor, Peyton tore up the rotten carpets and gave the subterranean venue a new lease of life.

From a discreet entrance on Glasshouse Street a sweeping stairway leads into the cavernous gold, red and marble lobby with its glittering chandelier. From here one can go into the grand dining room (a high, coffer-ceilinged room with horseshoe-shaped bar), to Dick's Bar (a timber-panelled room with subdued lighting and deep velvet armchairs), or to Chez Cup (another, more swinging, cocktail bar). The features of Chez Cup, originally launched in 1926, have been reinstated (not restored as is sometimes suggested). Circular in plan, the walls and textiles are decorated in a broad horizontal stripe of chocolate brown and cream, and the parquet floor continues this theme. Never before will you have experienced the sensational effect of being inside a chocolate gateau …

**David Connor 1994**

**David Connor 1994**

David Connor's approach to the design describes his attitude towards the project as a whole. He has tried to create a place where people can come and drink their first cocktail and never forget it, or just hang out and have a beer and feel grand. He speaks with a nonchalant flamboyance about his dislike of things or places that are too precious, slick or fussy; he prefers them to be daring and perhaps slightly vulgar. He is more interested in talking about the success of the Atlantic as a place for idlers and loungers, cool, straight and regular chaps – and girls – than about individual design details. They speak for themselves.

The budget was very small (an estimated twenty-fourth of Conran's budget for Quaglino's which opened at about the same time), and as a result Connor feels that the quality of some of the workmanship could have been better. Despite this, the Atlantic's restaurant and bars have been full to bursting since the day it opened, and have withstood the pounding. Fabric can be replaced, paint touched up, fixtures and fittings polished – so as long as everything is thoroughly maintained I cannot see that the champagne will fail to flow.

By the way, management assures me that the door policy at night is determined by fire regulations rather than a discriminatory bouncer – either way, it is very much in force.

ADDRESS 20 Glasshouse Street, London W1 (0171–734 4888)
CLIENT Oliver Peyton
SIZE total area 744 square metres SEATS restaurant 180
OPEN restaurant: Monday to Friday, 12.00–15.00, 18.00–24.00; Sunday, 19.00–22.30 (last orders 22.30). Bar: Monday to Saturday, 12.00–03.00; Sunday, 18.00–22.30 (last orders 22.30)
UNDERGROUND Piccadilly Circus

**David Connor 1994**

# Nobu

The restaurant is the first European venture for Japanese chef Nobuyuki Matsuhisa (his other restaurants are in Los Angeles and New York). A table at Nobu must be one of the most sought-after places in London right now. To give you an indication of its popularity, when I rang five days in advance for a Monday night the only available table was at 9pm. (Because it also serves as the Metropolitan Hotel's restaurant, a certain proportion of the tables are kept available for guests.)

Nobu is filled mainly with large groups. An international crowd of the most immaculately dressed (Prada, Gucci, Audrey Ang), porcelain-complexioned gods and goddesses swan in and out, looking very expensive, very chic, very relaxed. They seem to have been styled specifically for the space, which itself is the *pièce de résistance* of their outfit, the perfectly discreet accessory. The staff are dressed by Comme des Garçons.

The restaurant is a long low-ceilinged white room situated at first-floor level. Access is adjacent to the hotel lobby. Wide stone steps lead up to a small bar area at one end of the room – of note for its superb glass-fronted wine refrigerators. The main space is broken along its length by solid partitions (which act as service stations) to create more intimate spaces either side of a clear central route. The exterior wall features a continuous band of glazing with a return around the bar area. The view out is of tree foliage, with Park Lane and Hyde Park beyond. A frieze of etched-glass screens forms the internal wall at the back of the space and creates a corridor for access to the lifts, kitchens and lavatories. Floors are creamy Avorio Scura marble. Tables with oak and maple parquet tops on aluminium bases contrast with low-ladder chairs of oriental design and proportions. At the far end of the restaurant is a sushi bar. The only redeeming feature of this particular non-event in airport styling is that it exposes the sushi chefs at work in their preparation area.

**United Designers 1997**

**United Designers 1997**

Food is served on a variety of sumptuous props. For instance, the sushi arrives in red lacquered bowls, bulbous in form like one of the Michelin man's spare tyres. Most exquisite of all is the ice-cold sake served from bamboo flasks. (The cavity between two joints in the bamboo stem contains the liquid, which is poured from a small hole over a precisely cut lip into bamboo thimbles.) The green and fibrous bamboo is at its most exotic when the condensation begins to pour down its sides, and then, for a brief moment … you are in the tropics. Needless to say, the food itself is perfection and compellingly interactive.

Nobu has a mild elegance which incorporates the purity and quality of materials inherent in traditional Japanese design and cuisine. It is a Mr Chow's (151 Knightsbridge, SW1, established 1968) for the 1990s. Mr Chow possessed a unique flair and sensitivity, not only as a patron of the arts (he commissioned renowned artists and designers to make everything in his restaurants, from matchboxes to light fittings), but also as an innovative restaurateur, combining traditional Chinese cuisine with classic Italian service. Nobu follows closely in his cosmopolitan footsteps.

ADDRESS 19 Old Park Lane, London W1 (0171–447 4747)
CLIENTS/OWNERS include Robert de Niro, Drew Nierporent, Mr and Mrs Ong
SIZE approximately 300 square metres
SEATS 160
OPEN Monday to Friday, 12.00–14.15; Monday to Saturday, 18.00–22.15 (last orders 22.15); Sunday, 18.00–21.45 (last orders 21.45)
UNDERGROUND Hyde Park Corner, Green Park

**United Designers 1997**

**United Designers 1997**

# in-store eating

# 5th Floor at Harvey Nichols

A department store used to be a convenience shop for elderly ladies, where they could purchase a winter coat, a garden trowel and bar of lavender soap all under one roof. That was until Harvey Nichols relaunched itself in the 1980s as *the* department store for all the bright young (and not so young) things of Kensington and Chelsea. It continues to attract a youngish audience and stocks contemporary lines in fashion, make-up and home decoration as well as redefining window displays for the 1990s (although they seem to have lapsed in originality recently). The store is a 3-D version of a glossy fashion magazine.

The foodies' wonderland which is the 5th Floor at Harvey Nichols completes the shopaholic's day out, comprising a supermarket, café/ brasserie, cocktail bar and restaurant. The original concept was born out of a brief to refurbish the top floor of the store. Customers emerge by escalator from the main store into the central market place and a café. Since 1998 this area has been reorganised to include an espresso bar and a conveyor-belt sushi bar by YO!Sushi (see page 10.26). Overhead, the ceiling is partially covered by the 1970s roof structure which is made of triangular steel lattice beams covered with a pleated skin of acrylic diffusing panels and yellow-painted steel panels. The skin allows natural light to filter into the central area.

The north side accommodates the supermarket, which supplies everything edible – as long as it's esoteric. The wine shop on the west side also acts as cellar to the bar and restaurant, which are separated from the central space by a glass screen, making them independently accessible after shopping hours via elevators connected directly with street level.

All furniture and fittings were designed or otherwise specified by Wickham & Associates: the plywood Pola chairs in the café and restaurant and the cake stands and ice buckets with ball feet are Wickham's

**Wickham & Associates Architects 1992**

in-store eating

**Wickham & Associates Architects 1992**

trademark and emerge in each of his restaurant designs (see pages 1.24 and 4.8).

The design captures the activities of the street and bringing them up to roof level. Customers are given the opportunity to enjoy the view of the Knightsbridge skyline (rather than choke on the congested highway below), and to indulge in all the earthly pleasures that Harvey Nichols has to offer, and, more importantly, to be seen doing it.

ADDRESS Knightsbridge, London SW1 (0171–235 5250)
CLIENT Harvey Nichols
STRUCTURAL ENGINEER Whitby & Bird
BUDGET £5.4 million
SIZE 3000 square metres
SEATS restaurant 110, café 130, bar 70
OPEN restaurant: Monday– to Friday, 12.00–15.00, 18.30–23.30;
Saturday, 12.00–15.30, 18.30–23.30; Sunday, 12.00–15.30.
Café: Monday to Saturday, 10.00–22.30; Sunday, 12.00–18.00.
Bar: Monday to Saturday, 11.00–23.00; Sunday, 12.00–18.00
UNDERGROUND Knightsbridge

**Wickham & Associates Architects 1992**

# Thomas Goode

Baldassare La Rizza has had a career as exotic as his name. Born in Italy, he lived in France and Belgium before coming to London in his early 30s. After a mere 10-week course in interior design, he soon landed a job with interior designer Alistair Colvin, and then his own commission – to design the restaurant at Thomas Goode.

Thomas Goode is recognised as the most famous china, glass and silverware shop in the world, and is well worth a visit. Established in 1827, it moved to these premises in 1845. Thomas Goode's son William (an accomplished ceramic artist) joined the business in 1857 and commissioned architects Ernest George Peto to design a new frontage for the shop. The plans were submitted to Queen Victoria for her approval. A year later new galleries and 12 showrooms were opened, decorated with Baccarat and St Louis chandeliers and magnificent table settings. One particularly enchanting room was decorated in the Arts and Crafts style. An unusual feature and rare piece of Victorian design is the mechanical front door which opens automatically when someone stands on the mat. It is believed to be the last working example in the world.

One cannot help but feel like a crazed bull in a china shop when faced with glassware so fine that just one breath might reduce it to fairy dust. It so happened that on the day of my visit General Colen Powell of the US Army was having his picture taken in the 'plate room', beside the very bomb that hit Thomas Goode during World War II. The doorman held his gloved hands firmly behind his back and looked straight ahead as this enormous man (in stature and aura) picked his way between tables laden with foot-high champagne glasses.

La Rizza leans towards the lavish; he delights in luxurious fabrics, borders, gilt and rich colours. He was struck by the abundance of decorative gold detailing that embellishes so much of the glassware and china.

**Baldassare La Rizza 1994**

**Thomas Goode**

in-store eating

**Baldassare La Rizza 1994**

To encapsulate this detail, he based the restaurant design on a gold damask curtain fabric; he then commissioned the gold stencilled walls (built up with eight layers of paint), glass wall-sconce lights (made in one of the Thomas Goode workshops), and a small bar. Knowing that the British climate can invariably be dull, La Rizza chose warm dusky pinks and blues for the chair upholstery to contrast with the gold. The overall result is somewhat muted, as if any intensity of colour has been washed out by the rain. Because of the old gold in the curtains and walls, the room does not glisten, but gives off a restrained glow befitting its location and clientele. Although some details, such as the custom-made deep fringing on the chairs, have been exaggerated, the palette of colours is rather lack-lustre.

Table settings worth £250,000 from the shop were put aside for the restaurant, the idea being that the pattern will change with the seasons. Knowing this, strangely enough, makes one's dining experience all the more pleasurable. You will be spoilt by impeccable service and feed on light seasonal dishes, all appropriately served in a rococo style. I defy anyone not to thoroughly enjoy lunch or tea amidst the nostalgia of these hushed surroundings.

ADDRESS 19 South Audley Street, London W1Y 6BN (0171–409 7242)
CLIENT Thomas Goode & Co. Ltd
BUDGET £100,000
SIZE 35 square metres
SEATS 36
OPEN Monday to Friday, 12.00–15.00, 16.00–18.00. Private functions from 18.00 every day
UNDERGROUND Green Park

**Baldassare La Rizza 1994**

Thomas Goode

in-store eating

**Baldassare La Rizza 1994**

# Villandry

Villandry marks a sea change in the way Londoners can experience the buying, preparation and consumption of food. The original and much smaller grocery shop and café opened in 1988 in Marylebone High Street. The front of the shop was densely packed with the most perfectly selected produce from around the world and customers would be enticed into the back to sit at cosy tables and eat delectable snacks. A visit was like exploring inside the Carrarinis' own tantalisingly well-stocked kitchen cupboard and then being invited to stay for lunch. Even in the shop's infancy, the idea behind it was absolutely clear. The Carrarinis wanted to offer a range of products hand-picked for their excellence (each bearing a label relating the story of their origin) rather than a generic package which would inevitably result in the marketing of a particular lifestyle.

It is hard to imagine how such an intimate activity can be translated to a larger scale yet retain its sensitivity and high level of connoisseurship. However, the masterful team that is Villandry have taken this shift in their stride, and us with them. The new shop and restaurant reintroduce a way of shopping and eating more akin to the provision merchants of the late 19th century, when the likes of J Sainsbury offered 'the choicest butters of absolute purity ... Wiltshire and Irish bacon ... Gorgonzolas of the finest quality ... Egyptian quails ... Bordeaux pigeons' – produce that Villandry would be proud to stock.

Methods of displaying the produce are not dissimilar either. The Sainsbury store in Croydon circa 1900 'was elegantly fitted with mahogany, the walls being lined with tessellated tiles, and marble slabs and counters giving to the whole an inviting air'. Counters were at waist height with goods piled up on open display (not concealed behind huge sloping glass screens), and stools were placed at strategic points along the counters so one could sit and sample specialities. The shop at Villandry has specially

**Gavin Monk 1997**

**Gavin Monk 1997**

designed thick-set counters (fabricated in Leeds) made of English oak with either beech or stainless steel tops, and large oak Welsh dressers which cleverly incorporate chilled counters. The size and weight of the furniture has been inspired by the great kitchens of England's country houses and hotels. In the restaurant, the smaller, simple oak tables with copper bands around their top edges are copies of a design made for the kitchens at the Brighton Pavilion.

The products are arranged in a logical way that helps one to think about preparing meals (chutneys and mustards, for example, are placed near the cheese and meat), as opposed to all jars in one area and all fresh produce in another as in conventional supermarkets. The procession through the space is the key to the spectacle and practicability of Villandry. The main entrance to the shop is through fully-glazed double doors on Great Portland Street. The floor area occupies the full depth of the block and is divided into front, middle and rear bays. A central aisle (as found in the covered markets of many Italian and French cities) draws the visitor past cake stands, meat counters and wine racks into the restaurant at the back and to an exit on to Bolsover Street.

The basement is given over to the kitchens, including a wood-burning stove and a specialist pastry kitchen which makes all the bread for the shop and restaurant. Although vast distances need to be covered between kitchen and dining room, there is no dumb waiter. Food is handed over by the chef to a 'runner' (in long bibbed apron) who then flies swiftly up the generously sweeping scullery stairway to deliver the dish to the table.

Cloakrooms are also in the basement, and are again generously proportioned. All the fittings and ceramics were salvaged from the Mason's Lodge in Aldwych, built at around the same time as this building (c. 1900). Materials and colours throughout were chosen for their innate

**Gavin Monk 1997**

**Gavin Monk 1997**

qualities, enhancing light and texture. The walls are sealed grey plaster (from Ireland – English plaster is pink). Walls elsewhere are painted creamy white, softened by impeccable timber detailing and discreet indirect light sources. The copper wall sconces in the restaurant (designed by Mark Kirkeley) were brought from the original shop. Their shape is reminiscent of the plates and cups traditionally displayed on Welsh dressers.

The quality of the design and craftsmanship at Villandry appears to be peculiarly British, although it is the result of a more eclectic plan. Monk is Canadian (but studied for some time at the Architectural Association in London), Monsieur and Madame Carrarini are Parisian and South African respectively. This mix may explain the unusually relaxed atmosphere which emanates from the large store and restaurant. There are plans to open a bar in the 'south room' – but all in good time.

ADDRESS 170 Great Portland Street, London W1 (0171–631 3131)
BUYERS/CHEFS/CO-OWNERS Gavin Monk, Jean Charles Carrarini and Ros Carrarini
SIZE ground floor and basement 1100 square metres
SEATS 90
OPEN Monday to Saturday, 7.30–11.45, 12.30–15.00, 19.30–22.30; Sunday, 11.00–16.00 (single menu brunch)
UNDERGROUND Great Portland Street

**Gavin Monk 1997**

**in-store eating**

**Gavin Monk 1997**

# rooms with views

# OXO Tower Wharf

Originally built at the turn of the century as a post-office generating station, the building was extensively remodelled between 1928 and 1930 to serve as a meat warehouse for the manufacture of Oxo cubes. The strategic site and art-deco tower (designed by A W Moore) were chosen to overcome restrictions on advertising along the river. From its situation on the South Bank, Oxo could promote its products across a wide east/west panorama, from the City to the Houses of Parliament.

In 1993 work started on a scheme to transform the building into a large-scale mixed-use development. The first three floors are allocated to craft workshops and retail units, and there is a café on the second floor designed by Apicella Associates. The next five floors provide 78 flats for the Coin Street Secondary Housing Association, and the entire top floor is given over to the restaurant, brasserie, bar and viewing balcony. To accommodate all these different facilities within the one existing building three new cores were inserted: one at each end to contain the mass of the main structure, and one in the middle to provide elevator access. The north façade displays the original brick frontage and utilises old loading openings to create doors from each flat on to new metal balconies.

The intention for the restaurant floor was to literally lift the lid off the building, to proclaim a new identity for it and take full advantage of its location. A new aerofoil roof replaces the old slate and steel trusses and creates a double-height space on the eighth floor. Expansive glazing and a balcony now run the full length of the riverside elevation – a spectacular vantage point from which to look north across the river.

The elevator deposits you in the centre of the restaurant floor, from where you turn right for the brasserie or left for the restaurant. Little distinguishes the two dining areas except for the tone of leather upholstery on the Charles Eames wire chairs (grey/blue in the brasserie, black

**Lifschutz Davidson Architects 1996**

**rooms with views**

**Lifschutz Davidson Architects 1996**

in the restaurant). The floors are timber throughout and all the mobile furniture, waiter stations, wine coolers, trolleys and reception desks were designed by the architects (and made by Richard Becher Joinery) for this project. The fin-shaped display cabinets in both foyer areas pivot to direct circulation, rather like flood barriers. But most impressive of all is the louvred ceiling which shows white during the day and changes to ultra-marine at night, creating a most dramatic shift in mood. As well as varying light levels, the louvres are alleged to control acoustic reverberations within the lofty space, although I am not convinced that this works.

The north face of the building is permanently veiled in shadow. On a dull day, it can be quite glacial up there (the same could be said of the service). Strangely, the plan of the restaurant shares this single orientation rather than taking full advantage of 360-degree views. However, when I visited the brasserie for lunch on a hot and muggy August day, I was grateful to be able to sit out on the balcony and catch a cool breeze. The menu weighed heavily in favour of starters – a considerate response to the climate and dietary needs of its svelte and suited clientele.

ADDRESS Oxo Tower Wharf, Barge House Street, London SE1 (0171–803 3888)
CLIENT Harvey Nichols Restaurants Ltd
ENGINEER Buro Happold
SIZE 1390 square metres SEATS brasserie 120, restaurant 120
OPEN brasserie: Monday to Saturday, 12.00–15.00, 17.30–23.00; Sunday, 12.00–15.00, 18.00–22.30. Restaurant: Monday to Friday, 12.00–15.00, 18.00–23.00; Saturday, 18.00–23.00; Sunday, 12.00–15.00, 18.30–22.30
UNDERGROUND Waterloo, Blackfriars

**Lifschutz Davidson Architects 1996**

**Lifschutz Davidson Architects 1996**

# The People's Palace

The Royal Festival Hall was conceived, designed and built between 1949 and 1951 for the Festival of Britain by what was then the London County Council Architects Department (Robert Matthew, J Leslie Martin, Edwin Williams and Peter Moro). It was extended in 1962 by Sir Hubert Bennett. This Grade 1 listed landmark on the river is now the only reminder of that great event. It still stands out today as one of the best modern public buildings in London.

The People's Palace is located above the main foyer and occupies the entire 36-metre-wide frontage, affording spectacular views across the Thames. There has always been a restaurant here, but the new design set out to achieve a number of things. Over the years the original volume of the space and the central kitchen core (which backs on to the foyer) had been lost in a maze of partitions and stud walls. These were removed and the kitchen reinstated, with 4-metre-wide entrances either side. Materials and shapes throughout were chosen to draw on the language used in the original foyers and auditorium. Thus, a large screen-cum-canopy echoes the sycamore canopy in the auditorium and creates a focal point in the room for the central bar and entrance to the kitchens; and the slotted pattern in the plywood surfaces is reminiscent of the music stands and auditorium balconies. The carpet is a scaled-down version of the original design but in softer colours. A wooden edge at the perimeter of the room creates a boundary around the expanse of pattern.

The architects have introduced new elements, but they have a 1950s feel, such as the hanging hole-punched light fittings. The chairs (some wooden, some upholstered) by Vico Magistretti are faintly reminiscent of the chairs from the original restaurant designed by Robin Day.

The re-opening of this previously forgotten part of the building provides concert-goers with a dramatic way to begin or extend an

**Allies & Morrison 1995**

evening's entertainment. It revives a sense of occasion which was missing from the days when a pre-theatre dinner meant a packet of crisps and a soggy sandwich at one of the kiosks downstairs. Unlike the building, the menu in the restaurant has not been listed, and it has been influenced by a more contemporary style of sophistication – prawn cocktail and *coq au vin* have been replaced by chorizo and warm potato salad, and pan-fried mullet with saffron cream.

The room, with its spectacular scale and proportions, is a unique example of its period. It might have been interesting to see more original features reintroduced, rather than adapted. For example, there are few rooms in London which could show off a large patterned carpet in the way that this one could.

ADDRESS Level 3, Royal Festival Hall, South Bank Centre, London SE1 (0171-928 9999)
ENGINEER Scott Wilson Kirkpatrick
CLIENT Joseph Levin/Capital Hotels Group
SIZE total floor area 888 square metres
SEATS 220
OPEN 12.00–15.00, 17.30–23.00
UNDERGROUND Waterloo

**Allies & Morrison 1995**

**Allies & Morrison 1995**

# Putney Bridge

Putney Bridge is the only entirely freestanding new-built restaurant in London. Its superb location, between Lower Richmond Road and the Embankment, offers the chance to drink and dine overlooking a spectacular and uninterrupted river view.

The building, on the site of a medieval pier, was originally granted planning permission in 1987. At this time it took the form of an exposed steel and glass structure with a tensile roof. Although this was welcomed by Wandsworth Council, it would have been a difficult building to let out. Then restaurateur Trevor Gulliver (The Fire Station, Waterloo and St John; see 3.10) intervened and worked with the owners of the property and PKS to develop the present building.

Putney Bridge is spread over three storeys: kitchen and services at basement level, a bar on the ground floor, and the restaurant on the first floor. The Borough's planning department wished to see a 'public' building, hence the decision to run York stone paving around the building and into the foyer. Also, the conical shape of the glazed double-height entrance, with full-height glazed sliding doors at ground-floor level, opens up views of both the riverside terrace and the top part of the building. The exterior walls on the Lower Richmond Road elevation are clad in panels of Cebastone granite. This mixture of granite and marble chippings has the indigestible texture of chicken-liver pâté. Although acting as a baffle to reduce traffic noise on the inside, the cladding also creates an anonymous and impenetrable streetside elevation. The first floor is constructed as a lightweight steel and glass pavilion set on a solid base (a monolith). All windows on the river side are tilted to prevent reflections of the interior spoiling the view. The roof, finished in pre-patinated copper on the outside and plywood on the inside, floats on open steel trusses, generously oversailing the main envelope to enhance the sense of enclosure and

**Paskin Kyriakides Sands 1997**

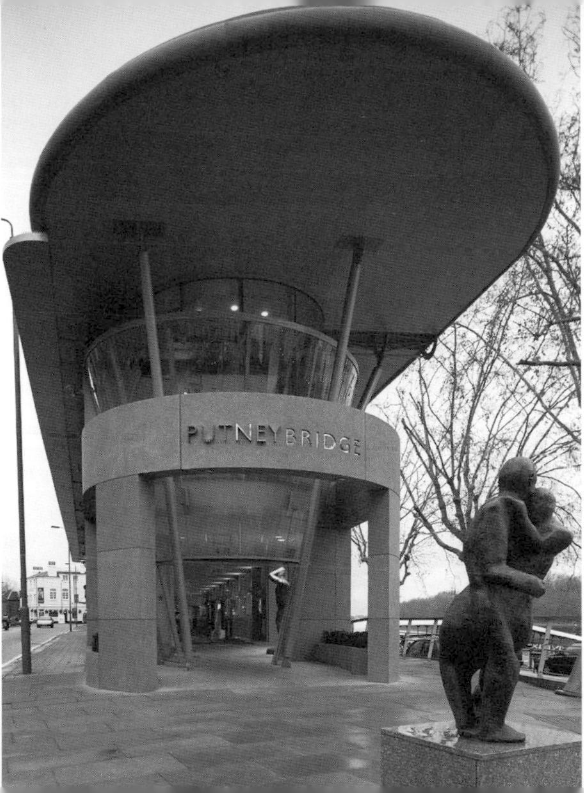
PUTNEY BRIDGE

shelter. It was originally conceived that the building would be naturally ventilated by river breezes. However, to ensure adequate ventilation in excessively hot weather, a 'raft' of air conditioning units was strapped to the underbelly of the roof. This unfortunately obscures the intended effect of sitting beneath plywood boat hulls.

The long and gently curving shape of the plan and interior design themes are loosely inspired by river boats and riverfront construction, encompassing also the idea of the durability and adaptability to the seasons of a houseboat building type. Timber is used extensively throughout the project, and is entirely reclaimed material. Floors and outdoor riverside terraces are laid in combinations of maple, iroko and Douglas fir.

An old sea-dog of a sculpted figure by Elisabeth Frink greets you in the ground-floor entrance lobby at the prow of the building, which leads directly into the bar. The bar itself is a thick wedge-shape like the hull of a boat. It is finished in makori timber and copper with a pewter top. The bar area widens and drops several steps at the western end to a polished concrete surface which can be hosed down on to the pavement – for those really busy nights.

The restaurant on the first floor is reached by a sweeping stair which takes you up to a small bar/reception. The best tables are to the right of the bar at the prow end of the building. Best, because they are quieter and less cramped than those in the main body of the restaurant, which is arranged on a split-level (to the left of the bar) to ensure good views for everyone. The outlook for all customers is the river and parkland on the northern bank. Due to this stunning aspect I barely remember what I ate on the night that I visited – it wasn't unpleasant, just undistinguished Modern-Ecu. Another minor distraction took the form of a duty-free

**Putney Bridge**

**rooms with views**

**Paskin Kyriakides Sands 1997**

display of plates near our table, which alarmingly turned out to be original Picasso ceramics.

The picturesque tranquillity of the river and its movements is not reflected in the atmosphere of the restaurant, which is hectic every night of the week. The tables are too tightly packed together considering the extremely high prices being charged (for a neighbourhood location) and the quality of the service. On the other hand, the scale and robustness of the bar is single-minded and functions successfully in its own right.

The site really comes into its own on University Boat Race day (early spring). With the starting line embedded in copper in the floor of the bar, it offers the perfect view of the beginning of the race – so perfect, in fact, that reservations are taken six months in advance.

ADDRESS The Embankment, Lower Richmond Road, London SW15 (0181-780 1811)
CLIENT Trevor Gulliver
INTERIOR DESIGNER Fitch & Company
SIZE total floor area approximately 870 square metres
SEATS 120
OPEN Monday to Saturday, 12.00–15.00, 18.00–22.45; Sunday, 12.30–15.00, 18.30–22.45
UNDERGROUND Putney Bridge

**Paskin Kyriakides Sands 1997**

**rooms with views**

# neighbourhood places

# Alastair Little

One of several West London neighbourhood restaurants where the chef/owner is as highly acclaimed for his cuisine as for his keen interest in design. Indoctrinated at an early age in the kitchens of Zanzibar (designed by Julyan Wickham and Tchaik Chassay in 1973), Little later became chef at 192 (see 1.22). On both occasions the architects worked closely with the owners in designing the premises (or were co-owners themselves) and with the chefs in designing the kitchens.

The restaurant is located discreetly at the end of a parade of shops running into a residential street. The brief, written with reference to a time prior to the contemporary fascination with lifestyle statements, called for a 'fashion-free' ground-floor interior. Bold architectural and graphic elements, quoting humorously from a romantic era, are combined with devices that are integral to the building: an over-sized dogtooth-checked awning marks the quaint shop front, and a backlit ceiling over the front dining area sits comfortably next to a skylight which runs down the left side of the compact space. The large embossed 'a' on the wall is more than just a logo; it is also reminiscent of the craft of typography.

The kitchen is in the basement and, being comfortably domestic in scale, can be visited on the way to the lavatories. In a similar vein to Stephen Bull's restaurants, the design is intimate and unique to its owner, reflecting his personal brand of creativity in the kitchen.

ADDRESS 136a Lancaster Road, London W11 (0171–243 2220)
CLIENT Alastair Little
SIZE ground floor and basement 140 square metres SEATS 40
OPEN Monday to Friday, 12.30–14.30, 19.00–23.00; Saturday,
12.30–15.00, 19.00–23.00
UNDERGROUND Ladbroke Grove

**Michael Merhemitch 1996**

Alastair Little

neighbourhood places

**Michael Merhemitch 1996**

# Euphorium

Owner Marwan Badran has embraced such diverse careers as working in the architectural office of Zaha Hadid and training to be a doctor. His current occupation is restaurateur. This may explain his adventurous approach to the design of his ground- and first-floor restaurant in Islington's Upper Street. The interior proportions and layout are reminiscent of the town houses in the area – small high-ceilinged rooms with tall windows and gardens at the rear.

The restaurant has grown and changed under the supervision of architects Munkenbeck & Marshall (also shareholders in the venture in lieu of remuneration for work done on the premises). The architects were initially brought into the project to make the small spaces bigger, and then ultimately to oversee the expansion of the premises within two years of opening.

One of the architects' favourite features is the 5-metre-high ceiling and conservatory frontage. The unusual height was found behind a false ceiling and created huge wall space for the display of paintings (all selected from Interim Art's stable of artists). By opening out the front, the restaurant interior is placed in the public domain and one's view is extended out and up. It has also formed a slim passage along the front so that circulation is not confined to the rear of the space.

This year has seen the complete transformation and expansion of the site. The front part of the restaurant is now an all-day café and bar with the back room reserved for the more formal restaurant opening out on to an internal courtyard. A bakery next door completes the Euphorium emporium.

A recurring theme in the new design is cherry pink. On walls, front window, menus and in the garden it is used as a navigational device among the more sober elements: stone floors, basket chairs in the café,

**Munckenbeck & Marshall Architects 1995/Dolswong 1997–98**

**Munckenbeck & Marshall Architects 1995/Dolswong 1997–98**

and grey felt chairs in the oak-panelled dining room. Badran continues personally to select art works for the restaurant with the idea that they should do more than just decorate the walls but provide a saturation of colour and texture that become integral to the overall three-dimensional composition.

Euphorium is entirely modern in its approach. Like the architecture, the service is cool and relaxed, and the menu, while it is traditional in its principles, flirts imaginatively with method, construction and budget – aromatic curry of pumpkin wafts past a £12.50 version of cod, chips and mushy peas.

ADDRESS 203 Upper Street, London N1 (0171–704 6909)
CLIENT Marwan Badran
ENGINEER Mr Badran (client's father)
BUDGET approximately £100,000 (original plan)
SIZE approximately 100 square metres
SEATS approximately 70
OPEN Monday to Saturday, 9.30–22.30; Sunday, 10.30–22.00
UNDERGROUND Highbury & Islington

**Munckenbeck & Marshall Architects 1995/Dolswong 1997–98**

**Munckenbeck & Marshall Architects 1995/Dolswong 1997–98**

# Granita

Until the 1997 election, Granita could not be mentioned without the epithet, 'the place where Tony Blair hatched New Labour'. Labour's triumph meant two things: the shadow cabinet had been enjoying an impeccable diet, and Tony Blair moved to Downing Street, leaving Granita to get on with its business in peace.

One can sense owner Vicky Leftman's relief. She is passionate about food and, it turns out, about her space too. Victoria is adamant that there was absolutely no design philosophy employed (I'm not sure that her architect, Tchaik Chassay, would agree) other than her hatred of clutter, objects and upholstery, which left her with an unadorned white box with timber floor and an unpainted rendered fascia surrounding the glazed frontage. She relents – John Pawson did advise on table tops. Since then the restaurant has undergone a minor facelift: the walls have been painted blue, perhaps as a way of embracing the new era, but probably because the restaurant is very much an extension of Victoria's home and moods do swing.

Sophisticatedly spare in design, the restaurant is extremely noisy – or rather its well-healed clientele is. The very deep plan and hard surfaces resonate like the inside of a megaphone. However, the food compensates with a menu covering all bases – meat, offal, poultry, game and vegetables.

The plan, with the bar tucked three-quarters of the way into the space, has been left as open as possible. Perhaps more could have been made of the bar in its own right – this is not one for sitting at.

ADDRESS 127 Upper Street, London N1 (0171-226 3222)
SIZE approximately 100 square metres SEATS 70
OPEN Tuesday, 18.30–22.30; Wednesday to Saturday, 12.30–14.30, 18.30–22.30; Sunday, 12.30–14.30, 18.30–22.00
UNDERGROUND Highbury & Islington, Angel

**Chassay Last Architects 1992**

**Granita**

**neighbourhood places**

**Chassay Last Architects 1992**

# Cicada

Australian-born Will Ricker decided that the highly energetic demands of running a restaurant induced a more favourable, even passionate, kind of stress than the kind he had experienced when working in the property business. Together with British designer Richard Gordon, he has transformed this 1950s building (formerly a bullion-smelting works) into a ground-floor restaurant and bar. More recently a private function room has been opened in the basement. A separate venture has converted former vault rooms on the upper levels into apartments.

Cicada sits in the centre of Clerkenwell, an area currently undergoing drastic change, both strategically and demographically. Since the 17th century Clerkenwell has been home to clock- and watchmakers, jewellers and gin distillers. Although many of the craftsmen survived until very recently, the location made it a natural overspill for the City. By the mid 19th century it had become filthy and overcrowded. Clerkenwell Road, as the main arterial road eastwards from the City, opened in 1878. It was part of the Victorian clearances which drove thoroughfares across acres of slums and quickly became a warehouse-lined tram route. It is currently under reconstruction in the Farringdon area, but when it reopens much of the traffic which presently runs around Smithfield Market and the Barbican will be redirected back along this route.

In keeping with the Victorian spirit which previously swept the area, many of the former warehouses are presently being converted into loft-style apartments for young professionals eager to adopt a Manhattan lifestyle. However, as is the way with city planning, the infrastructure (shops, newsagents, banks, etc) to support a residential community comes as an afterthought. A recent rash of change of use of buildings from industrial to restaurant indicates the shape that the area is adopting.

Preceded by Stephen Bull then by St John, Cicada is one such project

**Richard Gordon 1997**

**Richard Gordon 1997**

which appeals to a younger audience – it feels rather like a piece of west London in the east. Working with a rough industrial shell had its drawbacks, although it was solid in structure. One unforeseen adventure arose in the clearing of the basement – the former mercury-filled pit had to be thoroughly cleansed.

Ricker describes the interior and cuisine in digestible, bite-sized pieces: 'Frank Lloyd Wright with an Asian twist', with the 'warm, clean lines of early modernism' promoted by *Wallpaper** magazine. The design evolved on site; much of the work was hand-made and completed in situ, with the Asian influence creeping in later in the development. Gordon's ability to listen to his client's brief ('a pub but not a pub, modern but not too modern') and the dexterity with which he turns his hand to making anything – from a light fitting to a bannister rail to the sumptuous atmosphere of the basement 'opium den' bar – reflect the client's spontaneous and schizophrenic mix of styles and influences. The huge painted beetle which climbs the wall of the building is in the tradition of shop signage designed for an illiterate population, when trades were depicted by symbols rather than words. Perhaps this is also the most appropriate way to describe Cicada.

ADDRESS 132–136 St John Street, London EC1 (0171–608 1550)
CLIENT Will Ricker
BUDGET £230,000
SIZE ground floor and basement approximately 320 square metres
SEATS approximately 80
OPEN Monday to Friday, 12.00–23.00; Saturday, 18.00–23.00
UNDERGROUND Farringdon

**Richard Gordon 1997**

**Richard Gordon 1997**

neighbourhood places

# Polygon Bar & Grill

A new neighbourhood restaurant has been designed by a new young practice. More accustomed to designing very exclusive apartments near Bankside, Wells Mackereth have touched this small and inexpensive project with the same gloved hand.

To create a unified design, the exterior frontage of the whole building was transformed through modest means – render, applied timber panels and floodlights. The ground floor was previously occupied by a bookmakers. Simple full-height, full-width glazing at this level now exposes the bar and restaurant. The areas are separated down the length of the space by a screen which forms, on the right side, the high back of banquette seating for the restaurant, and, on the left side, a ledge in the bar area for leaning on. The division between the two areas is clearly marked by the use of materials applied to each. The tight budget demanded that materials be used inventively. This was achieved by using a backdrop of white walls and then combining the less expensive hard materials, such as the concrete bar, and steel counters and panels, with the richer hardwood floor and leather upholstery in the restaurant.

The *pièce de résistance* is the wall of orange-leather banquette seating which runs the length of the restaurant and beyond (by the addition of mirrors at either end). Bill Amberg, who supplied and dyed the leather for the wall, is better known for his exquisitely crafted leather handbags which, like the seat, are more than mere decorative accessories – they become integral to the visual structure.

Although it is fashionable at the moment to expose the kitchen area (the rotisserie is on display at the back of the bar), I'm not sure I feel the same way about exposing the wcs. Here, they are located at the back of the space, and I wondered whether the decision to paint them Yves Klein blue was an attempt to paint them out of sight. However, the lobby

**Wells Mackereth 1997**

**neighbourhood places**

**Wells Mackereth 1997**

provided between tables and WCs is not sufficient to shield partial views from one to the other. I am convinced that this can only be an oversight and that a small extension of the budget would allow the architect to address this fundamental problem.

The Polygon has many of the qualities that go towards making a good new local restaurant. The size and the layout of the single room is intimate but stylish. Food and service was satisfactory, if a little unsure of its footing. Prices are therefore over the top. Music would be greatly improved if turned off completely – the space is lively enough, visually and acoustically, without this extra intravenous dose of sound.

The architects' decision to focus on a few outstanding details has paid off; as a result there are areas of superb craftsmanship. There is also evidence of a feminine hand at work (Mackereth is the female half of this practice) in the treatment of the scale of the space as a whole. Tremendous teamwork must have been involved to get the project built in just eight weeks.

ADDRESS 4 The Polygon, London SW4 (0171–622 1199)
CLIENT Stuart Hopson Jones
BUDGET £130,000
SIZE dining area 75 square metres, bar 25 square metres
SEATS 75, plus 25 outside in summer
OPEN Monday to Thursday, 18.00–24.00; Friday, 12.00–24.00;
Saturday, 11.00–24.00; Sunday, 11.00–23.30
UNDERGROUND Clapham Common

**Wells Mackereth 1997**

**Polygon Bar & Grill**

**neighbourhood places**

# One Lawn Terrace

Financial adviser Nick Hall and his wife, Annie, an interior designer, are local residents and have small children – and lots of friends in the same boat. Until now the nearest place to go out to eat that in any way matched the aspirations of a young professional couple living in Blackheath was Conran's Butler's Wharf. A former print works provided the Halls with an opportunity to put Blackheath on the gastro-map, and within one year they opened One Lawn Terrace. The 1950s light-industrial warehouse suits the type of restaurant they wanted to create: a simple, spacious environment (welcoming to large families), with softer surfaces (light wood floors and stone-coloured fabrics) to appeal to discerning individuals. All furniture has been specially designed.

Although directly involved in the general day-to-day wellbeing of the restaurant, neither Nick nor Annie has a background in the restaurant trade. But they have surrounded themselves with specialists and professionals (who are also co-directors in the company: chef Sanjay Dwivedi gained his experience at Coast, Le Caprice and the Atlantic Bar & Grill, and general manager Raj Sharma was formerly with the Atlantic group.)

One Lawn Terrace is a sign of the constantly moving times. Today's light industry – the business of feeding people – is moving out of the city centre and into the suburbs, and with more than satisfactory results.

ADDRESS Blackheath Village, London SE3 (0181-355 1110)
CLIENTS Nick and Annie Hall
BUDGET £800,000
SIZE 440 square metres SEATS 150
OPEN Tuesday to Friday, 12.00–14.30; Monday to Thursday, 18.00–23.00; Friday and Saturday, 18.00–23.45; Sunday, 12.00–22.30
OVERGROUND Blackheath

**Annie Gibson-Hall with Gordon Russell of Detail Design 1997**

**Annie Gibson-Hall with Gordon Russell of Detail Design 1997**

# Great Eastern Dining Room

Restaurateur Will Ricker made his name with Cicada (see page 8.10) by breaking new ground in Clerkenwell. Since then he has moved even further east to Shoreditch, the domain of actors in the 16th century and today the home of the 'urban warrior': Thatcher's children are now in their thirties and the artists among them can earn a good living as designers in the multimedia-led companies which have made this gritty edge-of-the-city zone their home. The warriors wear combat trousers and all-terrain trainers to work instead of suits. One begins to see a pattern developing in the reclamation of such areas. As with Clerkenwell, manufacturing businesses move out to more cost-effective business parks and industrial estates; the first to take their place are artists attracted by low rents and the availability of light-industrial space; the local pub becomes colonised and outgrown so someone sets up a bar or nightclub to cater for 'their own' and the increasing numbers of visitors to the area; the area is thus redefined and put back on the map, the rents go up, the artists move on, and so on …

Today Shoreditch is comfortably on the edge of civilisation, boasting several independent bars, galleries and a cinema (The Lux in Hoxton Square). Ricker identified a gap in the market for good food. His private passion for Italian cuisine and a determination to make it affordable drove this venture. The premises are modest in scale (Ricker feels that there is a backlash against the mega site, divided equally between bar and restaurant areas. Australian designer Christopher Connell has used the formal elements of a traditional dining room to discipline the interior, combined with the air of sophistication that hangs over a Milanese restaurant, like the large bit of butter added to a plain sauce to give an appetising gloss. A chandelier (this one is made to an original 1950s Italian design), bitter-chocolate-coloured wood panelling (stained

**David Connell 1998**

**Great Eastern Dining Room**

**David Connell 1998**

## Great Eastern Dining Room

American white oak) and a wall mural of interchangeable posters by graphic designer Richard Allen transform a purely functional interior into a *propriétaire*'s fondant fancy. Ribbed glass in the restaurant window striates the light from the chandelier to create a fast-moving texture on the frontage while maintaining privacy in the dining room. Neon handwriting for the sign errs on the kitsch but is suitably understated.

Ricker's ongoing interest in promoting young artists and designers has prompted plans to open up the large basement as a viewing/club room for video art.

ADDRESS 54 Great Eastern Street, EC2 (0171–613 4545)
CLIENT Will Ricker
SIZE 540 square metres
SEATS approximately 90 (bar and restaurant)
OPEN restaurant: Monday to Friday, 12.00–15.00, 18.30–22.30;
Saturday, 18.30–22.30. Bar: Monday to Friday, 12.00–0.00; Saturday, 18.00–0.00
UNDERGROUND Old Street

**David Connell 1998**

**David Connell 1998**

# Konditor & Cook at the Young Vic

Konditor & Cook, the bakery (designed by Azman & Owens Architects), was established in nearby Cornwall Road in 1993 by *konditor* (German for pastry-chef/confectioner) Gerhard Jenne. His specialist expertise made the small bakery and shop immensely popular. The exceptional quality of its pastries, cakes and breads is an unusual find in London, let alone in this obscure corner behind Waterloo Station. The demand for space to sit down increased as the popularity grew, so when the café attached to the Young Vic Theatre became available in 1995, Konditor & Cook seized the moment.

The reasons for the success of the new business are threefold: firstly, its proximity to the original bakery (attracting existing customers with a new place to sit and a more extensive menu); secondly, its close association with the theatre (the café serves its administrative staff and actors during the day and operates as the theatre bar in the evenings); and lastly, the Young Vic street frontage (unlike that of any other theatre café/bar, attracting both theatre-goers and passing trade).

The footprint of the site is long and thin and set slightly below ground level. (The previous café on the site was dark and awkwardly designed.) Guided by a very small budget, interior designer Simon Stacey stripped the existing interior back to its shell state and then introduced a few key architectural elements to rationalise and enhance a fresher and lighter environment. In order to admit as much natural light into the space as possible, the street frontage is clear-glazed from end to end. The well-lit back wall of the room is solid and is used to full advantage for the graphic display of the café's name without obscuring the front window. Lone customers are drawn to the solid oak counter which runs the full length of the street side and reveals a view of endless pairs of legs striding past. The row of tables along the back wall is defined by a solid oak banquette

**Simon Stacey 1996**

**Konditor & Cook at the Young Vic**

**Simon Stacey 1996**

neighbourhood places

beneath the sign.

Materials and colours used in the interior reflect the generosity of the natural 'free-range' ingredients used in the high quality baking and cooking – walls are painted with double cream and the smooth marmoleum floor is like blueberry jam. Key practical features have been articulated simply, leaving room for decorative flourishes such as the goldleaf cake box in the entrance featuring Jenne's latest creation in confection.

ADDRESS The Young Vic, 66 The Cut, London SE1 (0171–620 2700)
CLIENT Konditor/Gerhard Jenne
BUDGET £20,000
SIZE 120 square metres
SEATS approximately 50
OPEN Monday to Friday, 8.30–23.00; Saturday, 10.30–23.00
UNDERGROUND Waterloo

**Simon Stacey 1996**

**neighbourhood places**

**Simon Stacey 1996**

# Konditor & Cook, Stoney Street

Records show the existence of a fruit and vegetable market on this site since 1276. By night Borough Market still operates as a wholesale market for shops and restaurants tucked underneath rusting sheds designed by H Rose in 1851 and extended by E Haabershon in 1863–64 and railway viaducts. It is one of the two markets in central London (the other is Smithfield meat market) which remains on its original site. By day, the area is a shadow of its former self – often used as a film set for tawdry crime scenes in detective programmes. That is until recently and a concerted effort by the London Borough of Southwark to utilise the empty space and to become known as 'London's larder'. Up until the 1960s a farmers' market was held on the site. The idea has been resuscitated, taking advantage of a growing scepticism towards the treatment of so-called 'fresh foods' sold in supermarkets, a wider availability of organic produce and a keener awareness of our indigenous foodstuffs and methods of cooking. Pie-makers, smokehouses and cheese-makers are just some of the producers who come from all over the country on the third Saturday of each month (call 0171-407 1002 for more details). Meanwhile properties in the immediate vicinity are being let to specialist food suppliers and manufacturers such as the Neal's Yard Dairy, the Monmouth Coffee Company and now Konditor & Cook.

K & C (not to be mistaken for KFC) is a rare mix of *haute-couture* patisserie and home-bakery. Jenne's theatrical cakes stand like primadonnas singing to an audience of adoring loaves of bread and enthusiastic cookies. The architects have responded by setting a stage to reveal all aspects of the operation in what is a very confined space. Everything is prepared and baked in kitchens at the rear and in the basement of the premises. The original timber floor and brick walls have been restored and then a few key elements inserted to organise and define

**Azman & Owens 1998**

**neighbourhood places**

**Azman & Owens 1998**

the shop space: a toughened-glass panel inset into the threshold reveals cake decorating below, a maple-topped shelf for the bread, an in-situ cast-concrete cash desk and long stone-topped counter lit from above by over-sized factory lamps, and a small glazed mezzanine office (unfortunately not a place to sit) propped on steel beams at the back of the shop. The controlled interventions are generous in mass of material and proportion but starkly understated in contrast to the flamboyancy of the product and its production.

The building conversion and its new occupant illustrate the process of boutiquification of urban areas which were formerly associated with wholesale trade and commerce (also occurring in other areas of the city such as Clerkenwell and Spitalfields) and an indication of what is to come in this neighbourhood.

ADDRESS Stoney Street, London SE1 (0171–261 0456)
CLIENT Gerhard Jenne
SIZE 180 square metres
SEATS 0
OPEN Monday to Friday, 7.30–18.30; Saturday, 8.30–14.30
UNDERGROUND Borough

**Azman & Owens 1998**

**Konditor & Cook, Stoney Street**

neighbourhood places

**Azman & Owens 1998**

# Sonny's

Barnes – always more town than country, popular with retired TV actors and musicians – has become a suburban haven for prosperous young families with large estate cars and dogs. Sonny's is a happy story which has adapted to the changes in the neighbourhood.

Husband-and-wife team Mascarenhas and Harris originally opened their modern European restaurant in 1986 to satisfy the sophisticated palates of the local media types (Olympic recording studios nearby still provides a healthy flow of hungry popstars and media attention). Basement kitchens were inherited from a previous restaurant on the site. Working with a very modest budget, the owners created a simple ground-floor interior to act as a backdrop for their growing art collection.

After 12 years of mechanical and logistical problems, the premises have been reorganised. The kitchens are now on the ground floor and a small backyard has been enclosed to create a larger dining room. A floor-to-ceiling terrazzo fireplace by Bruce McLean floats off a new glass-block end wall, creating a clear focus for the series of patched together rooms and floor levels which come with a conversion. This device has transformed what might have been a standard set of improvements into an elegant architectural statement. The warm fire set within its spirited surround against the daylit wall is also representative of the Mascarenhas's very personal view of the pleasures of eating in a restaurant rather than the anonymity of concept-led ventures.

ADDRESS 94 Church Street, London SW13 (0181–748 0393)
CLIENTS Rebecca Mascarenhas and James Harris
SEATS 100
OPEN Monday to Saturday, 12.30–2.30, 19.30–23.00; Sunday, 12.30–15.00
UNDERGROUND there isn't one in range; take a bus from Hammersmith

**Rebecca Mascarenhas, James Harris with Peter Radford 1998**

**Rebecca Mascarenhas, James Harris with Peter Radford 1998**

# retro-bistros

# Chez Gerard

Of all the restaurant chains in London which aim to put 'steak-frites' on the table, the Chez Gerard group creates the benchmark. With their successful formula – a consistently respectable standard of cooking, an educated wine list, and prices just below those of the so-called mega-restaurants – they are a cut above the likes of Dome and Café Rouge. The design and location of sites are key elements. Charlotte Street, Mayfair, Covent Garden, Chancery Lane, Bishopsgate, and now Islington (near Sadler's Wells) are all central and densely populated with businesses and places of entertainment.

Virgile & Stone's particular skill lies in their use of good quality materials and the specification of high standards of craftsmanship in individual details, coupled with their understanding of the consistent rigours of everyday operations. Here, 'a contemporary look' is combined with the romance of train travel and the traditional Paris café/bar interiors of the 1930s. The luggage racks fixed above tables and to the backs of banquettes – a simple and practical device for stashing coats and bags – have been adopted as Chez Gerard's signature feature.

Here at Bishopsgate, Chez Gerard incorporates the first Café Express – a quicker and cheaper way of buying into the picture, and appropriate for its proximity to Liverpool Street Station.

ADDRESS 64 Bishopsgate, London EC2 (0171–588 1200)
CLIENT Groupe Chez Gerard
SEATS restaurant 95, Café Express 50
OPEN restaurant: Monday to Friday, 11.45–15.00, 17.45–22.00. Café Express: Monday to Friday, 8.00–10.30, 11.45–23.00. Bar: Monday to Friday, 11.00–23.00
UNDERGROUND Monument, Liverpool Street

**Virgile & Stone Associates Limited 1997**

**Chez Gerard**

**Virgile & Stone Associates Limited 1997**

retro-bistros

# Bertorelli's

During the 18th and 19th centuries Charlotte Street was at the centre of an artists' quarter and home to some of London's most famous architects (including John Nash and Sir Robert Smirke). More recently the area has attracted the media set and, in particular, satellite-television companies.

Founded in 1912 by four Italian brothers, Bertorelli's was once the classic Italian place to eat, with the silver-domed trolleys, large cutlery and starched white linen that define a professional operation – and a dedicated family to give it personality. It was still managed by a family member until the mid 1980s, when it fell victim to the Kennedy Brookes style of management (see page 0.3) and the front part of the restaurant was relaunched as Café Italien des Amis du Vin, a concept to appeal to a younger audience, and entirely manufactured from start to finish. Meanwhile, the back room remained intact as a token of appreciation to an established clientele.

Recently, the whole interior has been completely overhauled and restyled for the 1990s. I would like think that this was done because the old place had become irreparable with age – but no, people apparently just don't want to go to places like that any more. Today's state-of-the-art restaurant has to yell at you from across the street before you will notice it, let alone want to go in. The strange thing is that the old hierarchy has been maintained in the new plan – the Café Italien now covers the entire ground floor, with the more expensive Bertorelli's restaurant and function room upstairs. A whole new space has been created in the foyer, where a palatial limestone and glass staircase with walls clad in carved oak beaver-tooth veneer masks the cloakroom and reception desk. At the back of the café a new atrium brings in natural light. Alterations to the street elevation enable a frontage of glazed oak doors to be opened out on to a new oak duckboarded terrace during the summer.

**Harper Mackay 1997 relaunch**

**Harper Mackay 1997 relaunch**

## Bertorelli's

Colours, shapes, spaces and materials have been combined and elevated to a hyperactive level of activity throughout. One such detail is the treatment of walls, which are finished with a woven lattice of veneered plywood strips of maple and American black oak. Their surface is punctured with coloured display cases which from time to time hold glass and ceramics on loan from the Contemporary Applied Arts Gallery. The effect is disquieting and uncomfortably temporary, like an exhibition stand at a trade fair. Spots of colour have also been brought out in details such as the green and blue water glasses in the restaurant, the red illuminated glass panel behind the bar upstairs, and the function-room carpet by Helen Yardley. No expense has been spared in the WCs – the sink unit in the Ladies is made from one angled slab of Calacatta-Vaggli Rosata marble, and the Gents features a urinal made from laminated and bonded sheets of glass mounted behind a water curtain.

If there was ever an argument for leaving something alone, this would be it. Yes, the old café was in dire need of a rethink and in many ways the front and foyer areas have benefited from the reorganisation. But the breadsticks in paper packets have been replaced by sliced sun-dried tomato bread in a basket. At the risk of sounding sentimental, the old Bertorelli's was a benchmark in London's restaurant history, and to have disposed of it completely is deeply regrettable and a tragic loss.

ADDRESS 19–23 Charlotte Street, London W1 (0171–636 4174)
CLIENT Chez Gerard Groupe
ENGINEER Howard Cavanna Associates
SIZE 372 square metres (total) SEATS restaurant 50, café 90
OPEN Monday to Saturday, 12.00–15.00, 18.00–23.00
UNDERGROUND Goodge Street, Tottenham Court Road

**Harper Mackay 1997 relaunch**

Bertorelli's

retro-bistros

**Harper Mackay 1997 relaunch**

# very fast food

# Belgo Noord

The Belgo concept is the creation of Anglo-Belgian Andre Plisnier and French-Canadian Denis Blais. Having been involved in restaurant and bar ventures in London since 1984, they set up Belgo Noord, 'the original moules house', in 1992. The idea was to introduce continental brewery/eating-hall culture to London by serving unpretentious, accessible and affordable food and drink in an architecturally stimulating environment. As soon as it opened its doors, Belgo was a sensational success. Much of the attention that it received can be attributed to the design of the original restaurant by anand zenz.

zenz (aided by architect Masa Garba) has created a completely original type of space out of a conventional site. The design was inspired by the concept of a contemporary monastic refectory. A deceptively uneventful, raw rendered façade faces the busy street opposite the Camden Roundhouse. A walkway spans the frantic and steaming kitchen with its tangle of ducting (the waste heat recovery plant) and takes you into the refectory, an unexpectedly deep and lofty vaulted room. Custom-made pickaxe chairs and robust tables are manufactured in zenz's own workshop from ash and oak (all farmed timber).

All wall surfaces are rendered. To distract the eye, and one's sense of humour, inscribed above dado height are medieval Rabelaisian names taken from the fantasy feast described in *Gargantua and Pantagruel* – Donkeythistle, Tasteall, Sweetheifer, Stickyfingers. (Rabelais was a 16th-century French satirist, noted for his coarse humour. He spent part of his life as a Franciscan monk.) At first, I thought they must be the names of the staff who, dressed in brown felt monks' habits, comprise another bizarre but integral part of the design. A favourite detail of zenz's is his treatment of the glass-block toilets, which are another event in themselves.

**anand zenz 1992/Ron Arad Associates (bar extension) 1994**

**Belgo Noord**

very fast food

**anand zenz 1992/Ron Arad Associates (bar extension) 1994**

## Belgo Noord

Eighteen months after opening, a new bar extension (designed by Ron Arad Associates; see Belgo Centraal, page 10.6) was built in the adjacent courtyard. The challenge here was to invent a roof which would enclose the space all year round yet maintain the feeling of being outside and allow natural light into the restaurant. The solution was a giant horizontal *brise-soleil*. Huge thin plywood beams frame double-glazed panels, both shading and reflecting light into the space. The supporting beams are swathed in graphite-coated plaster to blur the transition between walls and roof and provide casing for additional lights. Arad's relentless search for new ways of using materials and structures and 'inventing temporary visual vocabularies' is exercised here in his expressive freehand style. The design of the furniture is an important part of the pursuit: the bar is an amorphous stainless-steel counter (its base and the surrounding floor appear as one flow of concrete), and there are mirror-finished molecular table tops and mollusc chairs.

The original and surprising architecture perfectly complements the more traditional approach to feeding the masses – generous bowls of mussels and chips washed down with plenty of Belgian beer. Belgo Noord is eccentric and not to be missed.

ADDRESS 72 Chalk Farm Road, London NW1 (0171–267 0718)
CLIENT T R M Tisch Ltd
ENGINEER Bill Price of WSP Consultant Engineers
BUDGET £300–350,000
SIZE restaurant 160 square metres, bar 80 square metres SEATS 150
OPEN Monday to Friday, 12.00–15.00, 18.00–23.30; Saturday, 12.00–23.30; Sunday, 12.00–22.30
UNDERGROUND Chalk Farm

**anand zenz 1992/Ron Arad Associates (bar extension) 1994**

**very fast food**

**anand zenz 1992/Ron Arad Associates (bar extension) 1994**

# Belgo Centraal

Eating at Belgo Centraal is one of the most delirious experiences in London. Having entered the bowels of the 19th-century brewery warehouse, there is no turning back – you will become part of a futuristic underground culture and indulge (in a medieval kind of way) in the hearty consumption of mussels and chips and glass after glass of Belgian beer served by waiters in monks' habits. It is the second branch of the successful north London moules palace (see page 10.2).

Everything about the place is vast, elongated and frenzied. A 60-metre-long basement with brick vaults supported by cast-iron columns is host to a 200-seater beer hall (for a quick stopover seated on benches at long trestle tables), a 200-seater restaurant (for a more lengthy dinner at intimate tables), a 22-metre-long kitchen (where the chefs are all armed with pyrotechnical skills), and two 12-metre-long bars.

New street-level entrances have been created by removing three bays of the ground floor, forming a bridge connection between the two sides of the wedge-shaped building. The dissection creates a vertical foyer space to allow clear views down into the kitchens and up to the offices. A brightly lit industrial elevator has been slotted into the void to carry customers down in batches to the basement.

All the furniture and fittings have been designed and custom-made by the architects, embracing traditional functions while experimenting with shapes and materials. Shafts of light penetrate the basement through hole-punched surfaces to simulate the effect of daylight seeping through cracks in the structure. The toilets, with a fabulous communal washroom fountain, are shielded by a seemingly makeshift corrugated galvanised-steel screen: Glastonbury music festival meets Sellafield nuclear power station.

Each element of the restaurant has been designed to express the movement and process of the event and exaggerated to enhance the experience,

**Ron Arad Associates 1995**

**very fast food**

**Ron Arad Associates 1995**

taking the sombreness out of subterranean dining. Lighting has been used to ultimate dramatic effect, particularly in the lift shaft and along the kitchen. It is very noisy, but Belgo would not be Belgo without the backing track of pots and pans, fire, shouting chefs and raucous revellers.

ADDRESS 50 Earlham Street, London WC2 (0171–813 2233)
CLIENT Andre Plisnier and Denis Blais
STRUCTURAL ENGINEERS WSP Consulting Engineers
SIZE 1200 square metres
SEATS 426
OPEN restaurant: Monday to Saturday, 12.00–15.00, 17.00–23.30.
Beer hall: 12.00–15.00, 17.00–22.30
UNDERGROUND Covent Garden

**Ron Arad Associates 1995**

**Belgo Centraal**

**very fast food**

**Ron Arad Associates 1995**

# East One

Rodney Kinsman is more commonly associated with his furniture-design and manufacturing company OMK, and in particular with the company's work in airports around the world. His son Brandon has worked his way around the restaurant world, consolidating his position as co-owner and manager of East One.

The whole building on St John Street was already owned by Rodney Kinsman, but with the demographic climate beginning to change, and warehouse buildings being converted into apartments (see Cicada, page 8.10), the time was right to develop the ground floor of this strategic location.

The concept is inspired by the many visits that Rodney Kinsman has made to the Far East and his observations of the canteen method of cooking found in the factories and on the streets of China. The idea has been adapted to our sanitised post-postmodern setting. Customers select their own fresh ingredients from a deli counter and take them to one of the chefs at the 'wok station' – a purpose-built stainless-steel podium (designed by R Kinsman) containing several woks with a hood above to draw up the steam. Fresh running water from a fountain at the centre of the podium is used for adding to the cooking, to cool the surrounding surfaces during intense periods of cooking, and to clean the woks between batches of food.

As most of the kitchen is actually inside the dining room (only 20 per cent is behind the scenes; normally this would be about 50 per cent), the materials and furniture used throughout have been designed or chosen for their durability and low maintenance because they are easy to clean – 'modern but with traditional references'. The floor is terrazzo, the wall behind the deli counter is lined in small, white, swimming pool mosaic tiles. Long slatted timber benches divide the space horizontally, and are

**Rodney Kinsman 1995**

**very fast food**

**Rodney Kinsman 1995**

inspired by those found on the Hong Kong ferry. Tables with timber tops can be arranged in different configurations to suit small or large groups. Food is equally flexible: you can have just one bowl or a banquet.

The large and light-filled space is bordered on two sides by long horizontal steel-framed windows, and is uncannily reminiscent of an airport lounge (the bar tucked in the corner is the give away), but without the announcements over the Tannoy.

ADDRESS 175–179 St John Street, London EC1 (0171–566 0088)
CLIENTS/OWNERS Rodney and Brandon Kinsman
SIZE 300 square metres
SEATS 130
OPEN Monday to Friday, 12.00–15.00, 17.00–23.00; Saturday, 17.00–23.00
UNDERGROUND Farringdon

**Rodney Kinsman 1995**

**Rodney Kinsman 1995**

# Eco

At last it is becoming easier to find really good pizza in London to challenge the standard set by Pizza Express (since 1965). Really good pizza is the kind that measures at least 30 centimetres across and has such a thin crust that you could slide it into a record sleeve.

Eco is a gutsy attempt to create a contemporary pizza joint. anand zenz (architect of Belgo Noord, see page 10.2) knows how to get value for money out of a tight budget. He has the skill to manipulate the properties of materials so that all structural and decorative requirements and qualities are incorporated into the overall design.

Eco's flat rendered façade is the perfect antidote to the Sainsbury's video-wall frontage across the street. It forms no more than a hole in the wall and is conspicuous by its inconspicuousness. Inside, the space is a deep rectangular box. A low bar area (with rather nursery-school seating) in the front window is for waiting and lone pizza-eaters. An open kitchen with pizza ovens runs the length of the front section, with a row of tables opposite and steps up at the back of the space for 'no-smoking' tables. An enclosed mezzanine above accommodates the WCs and incorporates a domed skylight. This brings the notion of daylight into the rear of the space and illuminates the suspended cast-iron spiral stair access.

The room is lined in tough Finnish birch-plywood from floor to head height. The floor is an oversized chequerboard of black-stained and natural plywood sheets. The high-backed perimeter bench seating is made of 6-millimetre plywood, curved for comfort and to soften the impact of the hard-edged surfaces. The tables are 25-millimetre plywood, stained black and curved on two sides, with a pull-out leaf in each one so that tables can be slotted together for bigger parties. The high ceiling is also clad in rippling plywood panels which act as acoustic baffles. Above the line of the benches, the walls are rendered in rough concrete and left

**anand zenz 1993**

**very fast food**

**anand zenz 1993**

unpainted. Umbilical light fittings grow out of the walls, each one focused on to a table. zenz has brought his peeled-steel uplighters from Belgo to the no-smoking area. Reconditioned steel-tube and vinyl-upholstered chairs complete the neighbourhood diner.

A second, smaller, Eco was completed in July 1997 in Brixton Market Row, also designed by zenz.

ADDRESS 162 Clapham High Street, London SW4 (0171–978 1108)
CLIENT Sami Wasif
BUDGET £150,000
SIZE 250 square metres
SEATS approximately 80
OPEN Monday to Friday, 12.00–16.00, 18.30–23.30; Saturday and Sunday, 12.00–17.00, 18.00–23.30
UNDERGROUND Clapham Common

**anand zenz 1993**

**very fast food**

**anand zenz 1993**

# Pizza Express

This recent addition to the irrefutable Pizza Express chain is situated on the walkway inside Terry Farrell's 'air-rights' office block which spans London Wall, linking Wood Street on either side. If you work in this area, the arrival of Pizza Express provides some sort of comfort. As a visitor you are unlikely to stumble across it, even if visiting the nearby Museum of London, and will only drive at high speed beneath it. Once you are inside, there is no view as such, just too much window revealing the grotesquely oversized parts of the building overhead and the freeway below. For a change, one can forsake a view and relish the pleasures of a thoroughly unstimulating moment in the corridor between the City and the West End.

For more than 25 years Pizza Express has been as renowned for the 1970s flair of its interiors as it is for its pizza. An establishment with a less-marked identity could not transcend such an overbearing site. The restaurant is divided into two self-contained glass boxes, one on either side of the walkway, forming a new enclosure on a more human scale. One box contains the bar, the other the main restaurant, and each has a mezzanine level. The 19-metre-long and 5-metre-high interior glass façades create the focus for our attention. Supporting them are puzzling and bizarrely decorative steel and glass columns. Each one is made up of stainless-steel rods braced by 'dog-bone' struts and splayed arms which secure each 3 metre x 2 metre x 12 millimetre glass sheet at four points. Star-shaped bronze washers negate the need to countersink holes at these junctions. The glass sheets hang from a flange in the concrete-slab ceiling, which has a rotating steel arm fixed to a pivot joint. This detail forms the top of the column and takes up movement in the building's concrete structure. Stacked between the dog-bone struts are cast-glass isolators (usually seen on electricity pylons). Each one can withstand a load of 18

**Cantos Architects (restaurant); Bere Associates (glass wall) 1997**

**Cantos Architects (restaurant); Bere Associates (glass wall) 1997**

tonnes. At the bottom of the wall the glass sits in a stainless-steel channel and the column of steel rod and cast-glass disappears through a small steel foot.

It is an achievement that an original aesthetic has been born out of a structural solution, although the beauty of all-glass construction is obscured by the very elaborate columns. (The Channel Four HQ on Horseferry Road, designed by Richard Rogers Partnership, has a comparably complex treatment of glass.) I find the gently curved wall with inset glass revolving doors a more satisfying feature.

As an interior and an eating experience this branch is like any other Pizza Express you care to mention – including those in more readily accessible places.

ADDRESS 125 London Wall, Alban Gate, London EC2 (0171–600 8880)
CLIENT Pizza Express
STRUCTURAL ENGINEER Campion & Partners
SIZE total floor area 363 square metres
SEATS 240
OPEN Monday to Friday, 11.30–22.00 (last orders 22.00); Saturday and Sunday, 11.30–20.00
UNDERGROUND Moorgate, St Paul's

**Cantos Architects (restaurant); Bere Associates (glass wall) 1997**

**Pizza Express**

**very fast food**

**Cantos Architects (restaurant); Bere Associates (glass wall) 1997**

# Wagamama

Since the first Wagamama opened in Streatham Street in 1992 (close to the British Museum, the Architectural Association and University College London) it has become critical to the diet of every architect, designer, artist and student in central London, providing generous bowls of good and inexpensive Japanese noodles served in simple canteen-like surroundings. The design reflects the essential quality and disciplined informality of the cooking while offering a Far Eastern high-tech (= high turnover) level of service – this was the first place where London had seen waiters punch orders into hand-held computers linked directly to the kitchen.

The original design concept at Streatham Street was outlined by John Pawson although finally executed by JSP Architects. Pawson's pursuit of a personal poetic simplicity inspired by his observations of Japanese culture is now synonymous with minimalism in architecture, a term often used to describe the Wagamama interior. Although the doctrine arose originally in America, theorising a trend in painting and sculpture during the 1950s (seen in the work of sculptors such as Donald Judd and Carl Andre), its more recent use describes a sort of aesthetic hangover cure, detoxifying the postmodern excesses of the 1980s. Now the term has been adopted as a label for a more self-conscious 1990s approach to lifestyle. Wagamama introduced an element of the concept into every Londoner's repertoire, opening the door to a barrage of imitators.

Attributes peculiar to Wagamama which emerged from the site in Streatham Street included the basement location within an office building, exposed kitchens, long refectory table and bench seating, and a permanent queue. Many of these elements have been adopted and some of the issues re-addressed at the second site here in Soho. As an architect, David Chipperfield also strives for rigorous simplicity in his work. The restaurant is laid out over two levels: an open kitchen and entrance on

**David Chipperfield Architects 1996**

**Wagamama**

very fast food

**David Chipperfield Architects 1996**

the ground floor with seating in a single large space in the basement. The street façade is made up of seven consecutive full-height windows. Part of the ground floor has been removed to create a double-height section so that natural light can pour into the basement and passers-by can see down into the dining area. A long entrance corridor is bounded by a cantilevered acid-etched glass screen on the street side and on the other side by a view into the kitchen over a solid timber and stainless-steel counter. This generous area provides more shelter and a more entertaining way to wait in line than at the first site. Solid single-length timber tables and benches (with shelves beneath to stash coats and bags ensuring that walls remain unadorned) are a successful Wagamama set-piece.

Food is served from a bank of anodised aluminium dumbwaiters lined up along the back wall. The opposite long wall is clad in warm timber, contrasting with all the other surfaces which are finished in crisp, cleanable materials: floors in grey terrazzo and main internal walls tiled with white glass mosaic and grey grout. The irony of the two large central columns is faintly amusing. Clad in red marble like the remnants of an ostentatious foyer in a City office block, they have an overwhelmingly monolithic presence.

In 1998 Wagamama opened a third branch, incorporating Wagamama Coffee, at 101a Wigmore Street (0171–409 0111), designed in what has unimaginatively become the 'house style' by Anthony Munn Associates.

ADDRESS 10a Lexington Street, London W1 (0171–292 0990)
STRUCTURAL ENGINEER Chan Associates
SIZE 608 square metres SEATS 172
OPEN Monday to Saturday, 12.00–23.00; Sunday, 12.30–22.00
UNDERGROUND Oxford Circus, Piccadilly

**David Chipperfield Architects 1996**

**very fast food**

**David Chipperfield Architects 1996**

# YO!Sushi

An edible *Generation Game* for the 1990s (for those who don't remember this Saturday-evening TV show, the winner would sit in front of a conveyor belt and view prizes passing by – they got to take home all the ones they could remember when tested against the clock). So it goes at YO!Sushi. This is not the first time that the sushi-conveyor has been seen in London but it is the first attempt to create a contemporary environment for this truly fast-food concept. The concept was devised in Japan in the 1960s and today is considered a low-priced, low-quality form of sushi, as the food can be rotating for hours. However, YO!Sushi's spontaneity and generous opening hours are seducing Soho's fashion/media/post-production inhabitants.

Other than the lighting there is no part of the restaurant that is purely decorative, the entire assemblage being designed for its practicality. A 60-metre-long conveyor belt winds through the large white space. Customers perch on comfortable bar stools at the cherrywood counter, and chose from a continuous parade of colour-coded dishes which are counted up at the end of the meal in order to calculate the bill. Simon Woodroffe is 'proud of the robotic drinks trolley' which was developed from scratch. It cruises around the room, slowly enough for you to swipe a bottle of beer as it glides by. The charming creature is made from a wheelchair base with stainless-steel top and does not require a tip. If you do want a little human interaction you can dispense your own water from the tap in front of you or ask one of the sushi chefs behind the conveyor for green tea and specials to order.

A continuous strip of suspended light track follows the line of the counter, made from a crowd-control barrier. Programmable spotlights (usually used for rock concerts), TV screens (sponsored by Sony Honda ANA) and technobeats to keep your digestive tract moving in time with

**Charles Rudgard and Simon Woodroffe 1997**

**Charles Rudgard and Simon Woodroffe 1997**

very fast food

**YO!Sushi**

the conveyor belt complete the hyper-interactive scenario that has appropriated this old furniture showroom.

YO!Sushi, since opening their restaurant in Poland Street, have taken their conveyors to the streets. A 'double conveyor' can now be found at Selfridges Food Hall, 'a circular conveyor megasite' is at 255 Finchley Road, and an 'island conveyor' at Harvey Nichols (see page 6.2). They have also devised the world's first portable conveyor with matching drinks robot which can come to you (for more details call 0171–437 0500).

For more conveyor-belt dining go to Moshi Moshi Sushi on the raised walkway over looking the platforms at Liverpool Street Station, for the ultimate in food-on-the-move. Also, check out T'su at 117 Walton Street for a Chelsea version of the same theme.

ADDRESS 52 Poland Street, London W1 (0171–287 0443)
CLIENT operated by Dellway Ltd/YO!Sushi (majority shareholder Simon Woodroffe)
ROBOTICS Brilliant Stages
BUDGET £350,000
SIZE ground-floor restaurant 250 square metres
SEATS 120
OPEN Monday to Saturday, 12.00–24.00
UNDERGROUND Oxford Circus

**Charles Rudgard and Simon Woodroffe 1997**

**YO!Sushi**

**very fast food**

**Charles Rudgard and Simon Woodroffe 1997**

# Noho

The food is fashionable New Asian and the plan of the dining room reflects an establishment which paradoxically combines 'fast-track eating with traditional restaurant comfort'. A bar and servery form the centre of the plan – a mirror at head height provides company for solitary customers. An indoor/outdoor dining area at the front is defined by a decked terrace giving way to oak flooring inside with a full-height folding shopfront to be pulled back in fine weather. Another mirrored wall in this front area reflects street activity on to the inside. The full-width skylight at the rear of the site floods a larger dining area with natural light. This space is softened by suede-upholstered light coves and perimeter banquette seating. Chairs throughout are a polyprop design by Robin Day but have been embellished by Softroom with suede seat and back pads.

Softroom describe themselves as 'an architectural practice and ideas agency … [they] design for real and virtual worlds'. Noho is the real-world manifestation of their ongoing series of design features for *Wallpaper** magazine which combine the practice of built architecture with an exploration of digital space. The result is unsurprisingly like the pages of the aforesaid magazine – a series of chic *tableaux vivants*.

While design and its execution have become increasingly sophisticated, combining concepts in art with simple architectural devices and employing a tastefully sensuous palette of materials, the distillation of such references becomes over-simple and indicative of a self-referential moment.

ADDRESS 32 Charlotte Street, London W1 (0171–636 4445)
BUDGET £228,000
SIZE 228 square metres SEATS 80
OPEN Monday to Saturday, 12.00–23.30; Sunday, 12.00–22.00
UNDERGROUND Tottenham Court Road or Goodge Street

**Soft Room 1998**

**very fast food**

**Soft Room 1998**

# AKA

First there was a nightclub called The End, then its owners and dedicated clientele grew up and needed somewhere more comfortable to hang out. Both the nightclub and now the bar and restaurant are housed in a former Post Office depot (linked to other central London depots by tunnels).

The scale of the original building with its high-ceilinged interior space suggested to the architect a few strong pieces. The ground floor is dominated by a long bar; an area for informal eating and drinking is defined by a continuous band of blue-velvet banquette seating around the perimeter wall. The rough facing wall with stencilled traces of postal areas has been left in its original state.

The huge volume of the interior required an intervention which in turn would create more floor space. Therefore the restaurant proper is located on a new mezzanine level. A special party table juts out into the void. The heavy structural and safety demands of the new floor give more of an impression of excavation than intrusion. This slick mix of industrial shell with black plastic Phillipe Starck chair (in the bar area) and movie viewings at brunch on Sundays puts AKA right at home on the Lower West Side of New York in the early 1980s: 'the nightclub' moves upstairs … and now it's OK to invite your parents.

ADDRESS 18 West Central Avenue, London WC1 (0171–836 0110)
CLIENTS Layo Paskin, Richard Brindle, Richard West, Douglas Paskin
SIZE approximately 350 square metres
SEATS capacity seated and standing of 250-300
OPEN bar: Monday, 18.00–1.00, Tuesday to Thursday, 12.00–16.00, 18.00–3.00; Friday, 12.00–3.00; Saturday, 18.00–3.00. Restaurant: Tuesday to Friday, 12.00–15.00, 18.00–1.00; Sunday, 12.00–18.00
UNDERGROUND Tottenham Court Road

**Paskin Kyriakides Sands with David Connor 1998**

**Paskin Kyriakides Sands with David Connor 1998**

# a world of their own

Momo 11.2
Moro 11.6
PukkaBar 11.10

# Momo

Momo, the restaurant, marks a new direction for food and restaurant design in London. There is a certain sameness in the modern style (regardless of flamboyant gestures) of many of the restaurants established in recent years, but lately a new and exotic ethnic style has begun to emerge. Momo, the proprietor of Momo, made Heddon Street fashionable with his Moroccan temple to the tagine (inspired by his admiration for the Egyptian modernist architect Hassan Fathy) long before Conran moved in with his Zinc Bar a few doors along (see page 2.24).

The front elevation suggests little of what lies inside. A pair of traceried doors lean against the innocuous office-block frontage. But once inside, you are in the bowels of a medina. Islamic architects from the 10th century displayed the whole structural system and its complex patterns of symmetrical arcs when constructing domes and arches, whereas the Romans concealed the framework inside the fabric. The former method – more intricate to construct – suggests a reason why Islamic domes and arches span only very small distances, producing a dense effect of multiple chambers. An architectural joke has been played with this idea in the ground-floor restaurant. Columns interrupt the space at regular intervals, except over the bar where just the column head remains.

The whole interior is actually an artificial lining, although this in no way detracts from the overall appeal. The walls are clad in delicately traceried panels. Their original purpose would have been to allow cool air to breeze through the walls, but here they have been used to diffuse artificial light. The remarkably small open kitchen – with apparently mud-clad walls and roof – is placed at the head of the space as you enter. Chairs and tables are authentically low (a most satisfying aspect of the design) and surrounded by Momo's personal collection of objects gathered from Algeria, Morocco, Egypt, Syria and Turkey. Some prove useful – earth-

**Danielle Holando, JFKA Paris 1997**

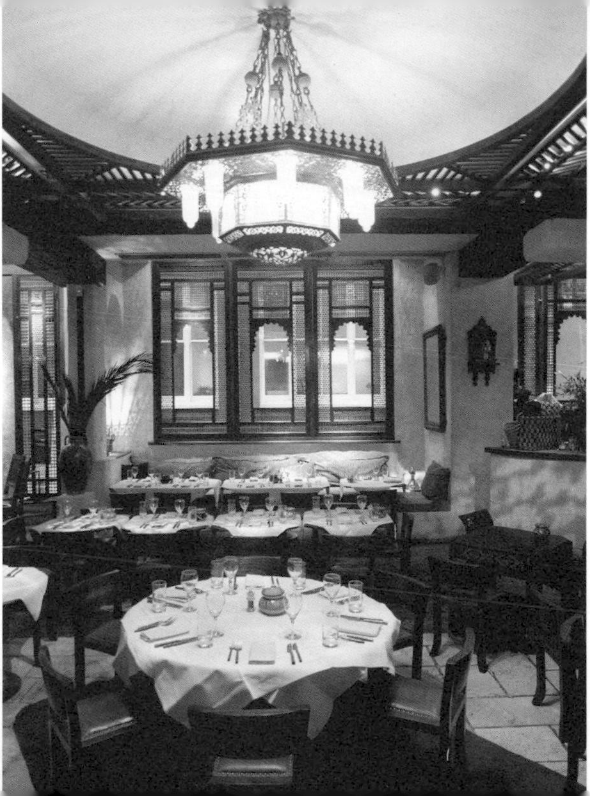

enware pots, plates and bowls, rugs and wooden chests full of cutlery – others remain purely decorative. The atmosphere intensifies in the basement bar.

To suggest that Momo is themed would be an insult to the eccentricities of its proprietor – the food alone is terrific. During the summer the pavement is appropriated as a surreal outdoor setting – huge rugs are rolled out and set with chairs and tables as if in the middle of a vast, light-filled room.

ADDRESS 25 Heddon Street
London W1 (0171–434 4040/434 2011)
CLIENT Momo
BUDGET restaurant and bar £500,000
SIZE 150 square metres
SEATS approximately 100
OPEN Monday to Friday, 12.30–14.30, 19.00–23.30;
Saturday, 19.00–23.30
UNDERGROUND Piccadilly Circus

**Danielle Holando, JFKA Paris 1997**

**Momo**

**a world of their own**

**Danielle Holando, JFKA Paris 1997**

# Moro

The unexpectedly exotic Spanish and North African aromas that pour out of the kitchen and colour the plates at Moro pervade a neighbourhood where previous generations of local residents have been more accustomed to frequenting the pie and mash shop a few doors down. With a new, younger population moving into the area to live and work, combined with the increasing desire of Londoners to explore the city in search of excellent food and new surroundings, Moro is at the epicentre.

A former Spar supermarket was razed to the ground and rebuilt in order to accommodate a restaurant on the ground floor with flats above. More space was gained at the rear of the site and to the side for bathrooms, storage and a small courtyard. The ground-floor area spans two bays, creating an impressive street frontage of horizontal, timber-framed sash windows (similar to those found in the cafés in Amsterdam), which can be opened up in the summer. In the winter, the double doors in the middle are shielded by a thick, heavy curtain which makes a draught-free lobby between the street and dining room.

The overall design is simple and explicit in its deep rectangular plan – undoubtedly inspired by time spent by each of the chef/owners in the kitchens of The River Cafe (page 1.14), and The Eagle (just around the corner in Farringdon Road). The main table-filled space with oak timber floors is all on one level, bordered on the left side by a 14-metre-long zinc bar at which one can sit for *raciones* (like *tapas* or *meze*). A wide opening in the back wall permits a direct view into the kitchen (with a wood-burning oven taking centre stage), and forms a counter-top servery so that food can be handed over directly from chef to waiter. The clients were insistent from the outset that the emphasis of the plan should be on the kitchen and the oven in which the chefs make all their own bread. A skylight overhead creates a comfortable and naturally lit working area.

**Alex Michaelis & Tim Boyd Associates 1997**

**a world of their own**

**Alex Michaelis & Tim Boyd Associates 1997**

**Moro**

The gently curved ceiling of the main space has been dropped to conceal ventilation ducting, and the continuous recess around the edge of the room provides a means of indirectly lighting the space.

Blocks of edible colour against the predominantly creamy walls hint at the culinary influences without attempting to ape a Moorish style. The spinach-green band which forms the back of the continuous bench seating along the right-hand wall is like a glaze on earthenware, softened by striped bolster cushions and consistent with the green-glazed tiling behind the bar and on the aubergine-coloured front elevation. While it is satisfyingly rudimentary in its requirements as a place in which to enjoy the preparation, cooking and eating of food, Moro succeeds in bringing all one's senses to life.

ADDRESS 34–36 Exmouth Market, London EC1 (0171–833 8336)
CLIENTS Mark Sainsbury (front of house), Samuel Clark, Samantha Clarke and Jake Hodges (chefs)
SIZE 230 square metres
SEATS 80
OPEN restaurant:12.30–14.30, 19.00–22.30. Bar: 12.00–22.30; closed at weekends
UNDERGROUND equidistant between Angel and Farringdon

**Alex Michaelis & Tim Boyd Associates 1997**

**a world of their own**

**Alex Michaelis & Tim Boyd Associates 1997**

# PukkaBar

To say that Trevor Gulliver is able to capture culinary moods in unusual locations would be an understatement. The man behind St John (see page 3.10), Putney Bridge (see page 7.10) and The Waterloo Fire Station has now turned his hand to Indian food in the suburbs. Not an attempt to be faithful to the many different kinds of food found throughout India, this is an essay in redefining the British-Indian version of 'a curry and a pint of lager'. PukkaBar turns the Indian restaurant as a venue for post-pub degeneracy into a place where families are welcome and the food is surprisingly good.

David Collins has wrestled with a charmless site in the middle of a post-war parade of shops and a strict budget which has determined a maximum-effect-with-minimum-expense approach. 'The effect' is tea-planter's lounge-cum-railway terminus, which contributes ideas on how the space might be used rather than the way it is finished. A timber-floored bar area with fake-leather armchairs and long library table precedes the curry hall with its tiled floor and dark wooden furniture. A wood-panelled dado, a sprinkling of ornate lanterns and the gentle whirring of ceiling fans create a ready-faded elegance. The upright chairs are satisfyingly heavy and compensate for the nasty floor tiles, and the library table is so deliberate in its purpose and generous in its proportions that it helps to overcome the general lack of charisma throughout the space, proving that it is more effective to delve into an architectural vocabulary than to impose unrealistic demands on a patchwork of inferior materials.

ADDRESS 42 Sydenham Road, London SE26 (0181–778 4629)
CLIENT Trevor Gulliver
OPEN Monday to Saturday, 12.00–23.00; Sunday, 12.00–15.30, 19.00–22.30
TRAIN Sydenham mainline station

**David Collins 1998**

**PukkaBar**

**a world of their own**

**David Collins 1998**

# index

# Index

**eat london: architecture and eating**

**eat london: architecture and eating**

# Index

eat london: architecture and eating

# also available from ellipsis

### london: a guide to recent architecture
Samantha Hardingham
A snapshot of London, with a wave of Lottery-funded projects and the Jubilee Line Extension designed by the UK's most exciting architects, while the Millennium Dome provides a controversial full stop to the century.
ISBN 1 899858 92 X

### dyke london: a guide
Rosa Ainley
Clubs come and go, homosexuality goes in and out of style, but the life of the London dyke continues. This guide suggests venues to tempt every-dyke, whatever level of (in)visibility you might crave, not ignoring the daily necessities – buying underwear, furniture, food, or make-up.
ISBN 1 899858 74 1

### gay london: a guide
William McLoughlin *et al*
More than a listing, this guide provides an insight to the many pleasures the city has to offer, from the pursuit of spectral figures in Abney Park Cemetery to the house of Frederic Lord Leighton, from clubs to classical music, and from Earl's Court to the East End.
ISBN 1 899858 73 3

### art london: a guide to contemporary art spaces
Martin Coomer
From the artist-run or alternative spaces of the East End to the blue-chip showrooms of the West End, and beyond, this is a vibrant and opinionated tour of spaces for contemporary art, encompassing the key personalities and most exciting exhibitions of the last few years.
ISBN 1 899858 75 X

PRICE £8.00